The Register

of

New Netherland

1626 to 1674

Edmund B. O'Callaghan

HERITAGE BOOKS
2008

HERITAGE BOOKS
AN IMPRINT OF HERITAGE BOOKS, INC.

Books, CDs, and more—Worldwide

For our listing of thousands of titles see our website at
www.HeritageBooks.com

Published 2008 by
HERITAGE BOOKS, INC.
Publishing Division
100 Railroad Ave. #104
Westminster, Maryland 21157

Copyright © 1865 Edmund B. O'Callaghan

All rights reserved. No part of this book may be reproduced or transmitted in any form or by any means, electronic or mechanical, including photocopying, recording or by any information storage and retrieval system without written permission from the author, except for the inclusion of brief quotations in a review.

International Standard Book Numbers
Paperbound: 978-0-7884-2226-3
Clothbound: 978-0-7884-7012-7

TO THE

HON. HENRY C. MURPHY,

LATE

UNITED STATES MINISTER AT THE HAGUE,

EMINENTLY DISTINGUISHED IN THE FIELD OF

NEW NETHERLAND HISTORY AND LITERATURE,

THIS WORK

IS RESPECTFULLY INSCRIBED.

PREFACE.

New Netherland, worthy Reader, may be truly called, The Mother of States, for her Territory extended originally from the Chesapeake unto Cape Cod. In course of time, however, the Connecticut river became her Northern Boundary, and so continued to be until 1650, when, by the Treaty concluded at Hartford, her bounds upon the Main were fixed at the west side of Greenwich bay, being about four miles from Stamford, Conn., and upon Long Island, at Oysterbay — the portion east of this last mentioned locality belonging to the English, and the westernmost part of said Island, to the Dutch. Thus, in fine, did it come to pass, that the present States of Delaware, New Jersey and New York are the legitimate and, we are glad to know, the prosperous offspring of our own New Netherland, which Henry Hudson, then in the employ of the Dutch East India Company, discovered, as our Annals show, in the Year of Grace, 1609, long before Plymouth Rock was known.

Colonization followed, and with colonization came Civilization, and with civilization, a regular form of government.

Who were the Pioneers in the mighty work of wresting this vast territory from Barbarism—who were they who first established Churches, Courts, Schools, and Hospitals; introduced Agriculture, Navigation, and the kindred Arts of civilized life, and thus laid the foundation of Institutions, which, multiplying in course of years, have since constituted the honor, the pride and the glory of the EMPIRE STATE?

Reader, the object of this little Book, which is commended to your patient indulgence, is to rescue from oblivion the Names of those brave and worthy Men. Their bodies

"are dust,
And their good swords are rust,
Their souls are with the Saints, we trust."

CONTENTS.

Advocates	122
Ambassadors	137
Annals of New Netherland	xi
Board of Audit	25
Book-keepers	25
Book-keeper's Clerks	26
Burghers, Great and Small	171
Burgomasters and Schepens	58
Clergymen	118
Reformed Dutch	118
Independent	120
Catholic	122
Commander of the Company's Ships	23
Commissaries of Accounts	25
Commissaries of Districts	47
Commissaries of Stores	30
Commissioners	150
Commissioners of New Amstel	6
Comptroller	25
Comptroller of the Windmill	25
Council	11
Conventions	140
Court Messengers	109

CONTENTS.

Directors of the Amsterdam Chamber	1
Directors General	9
Farmers of the Revenue	33
Ferry Masters	117
Fire Wardens	113
Indian Interpreters	133
Inspectors	115
Of Tobacco	115
Of Beer Barrels	116
Of Bread	116
Of Weights and Measures	116
Jailers	112
Magistrates	68
Matron of the Hospital	128
Matron of the Orphans	127
Measurers of Grain and Lime	116
Midwives	128
Millers	117
Naval Officer	23
Notaries	123
Orphan Masters	65
Overseers of Mechanics and Laborers	134
Patroons of New Netherland	7
Physicians and Surgeons	124
Provincial Agents	136
Provincial Secretaries	27
Deputy Secretaries	28
English Secretaries	28
Secretary's Clerks	28

CONTENTS.

Provost Marshals	111
Representatives of the Commonalty	52
The Twelve Men	52
The Eight Men	53
The Nine Men	55
Roy Masters	115
Schoolmasters	129
Schout Fiscals	38
Local Schout Fiscals	39
Surveyors General	37
City Surveyors	115
Town Clerks	103
Town Crier	112
Town Treasurers	109
Turnkeys	112
Vendue Masters	114

(B)

ANNALS OF NEW NETHERLAND.

1609. Henry Hudson discovers the North river, or the River of the Mountains, September 3d, and anchors near the site of the present City of Albany. July 30, Lake Champlain discovered. The Iroquois defeated some days after by Champlain near Crown Point.
1610. Another Dutch vessel visits the River of the Mountains, now called the River Mauritius, in honor of Prince Maurice of Nassau.
1612. Various vessels trade along the River Mauritius.
1613. Huts constructed on Manhattan Island and the yacht Restless built there.
1614. Fort Nassau erected on an island immediately south of the present city of Albany. The name of NEW NETHERLAND first given to the country. Long Island Sound explored by Adrian Block and the Connecticut river discovered.
1615. Champlain discovers Lake Ontario, and defeats the Iroquois south of it.
1620. Puritans in Holland apply for permission to emigrate to New Netherland which is refused. Capt. Thomas Dermer, an English navigator, visits Manhattan Island.

1621. Dutch West India Company incorporated; New Netherland included within its charter. ADRIAEN JORIS Director, or Governor.
1623. Colonization of New Netherland commenced. Fort Orange built. Fort Nassau erected on the east shore of the Delaware river. The Dutch take possession of the Connecticut river. Settlement of Long Island begun.
1624. CORNELIS JACOBSEN MAY, Director.
1625. WILLIAM VERHULST, Director. Horses, Cows, Sheep and Swine arrive from Holland.
1626. PETER MINUIT, Director. Fort Amsterdam on the Island of Manhattan, founded. Erection of a place of worship commenced on that Island.
1627. Trade opened between New Netherland and New Plymouth.
1628. Population of Manhattan Island, two hundred and seventy souls. First Clergyman arrives there.
1629. Charter to Patroons granted.
1630. Patroons' Colonies or Manors founded. Slavery established. Settlement of Renselaerswyck commenced. Staten Island and Pavonia purchased.
1632 Swanendael Colonie, on the Delaware, cut off by the Indians.
1633. WOUTER VAN TWILLER, Director. First Schoolmaster arrives. Trade opened with Virginia. First English ship called the William of London, ascends the Hudson river. Fort Good Hope on the Connecticut completed. A wooden Church erected at Manhattan.

ANNALS OF NEW NETHERLAND.

1635. Long Island conveyed to Lord Stirling. The English intrude on the Connecticut river. Fort Amsterdam completed.
1636. New Amersfoort, now Flatlands, L. I., founded.
1637. Settlements in Westchester and at the Waal-boght commenced.
1638. WILLIAM KIEFT, Director. Inspection laws introduced. Swedes settle on the Delaware and build Fort Christina. The Dutch Governor protests against the intrusion. Quit rents introduced in New Netherland.
1639. First grant of land in the present town of Gravesend, Long Island.
1640. Indian title to lands on Long Island, west of Oysterbay, extinguished. The English attempt a settlement on that Island under a grant from Lord Stirling, and are expelled. His Lordship's agent arrested. Free Colonies established.
1641. Settlement of Staten Island commenced. Wampum the general currency. Meeting of the Twelve Men convoked. Peter Minuit dies.
1642. The Twelve Men dissolved. War against the Weckquaeskecks, (or Westchester county) Indians. Newtown patent issued. Throg's Neck and adjoining lands granted. Erection of a stone Church in New Amsterdam commenced. English expelled from the South, or Delaware river. First clergyman at Renselaerswyck and Fort Orange. Father Jogues captured by the Mohawks.

1643. War with the Indians around Manhattan Island. Great destruction of lives and property. The life of the Director General threatened. The Eight Men elected. Father Jogues escapes from the Mohawks. First Church at Fort Orange, or Beverwyck (now Albany). Sir Edmund Plowden lays claims to the territory forming the present State of New Jersey.

1644. Hempstead, L. I., planted. John Underhill defeats the Westchester Indians. Peace concluded with several Indian tribes. First Excise laws enacted. Patroon of Renselaerswyck fortifies Beeren Island, opposite Coeymans, and attempts to levy toll on vessels passing up and down the Mauritius, or Hudson river; consequent conflicting jurisdiction.

1645. General peace with the Indians. Indian title to what is now New Utrecht, L. I., extinguished. Settlement of Flushing commenced. Town of Gravesend erected.

1646. Adriaen van der Donck founds a colonie near Spyt den Duyvel, under the name of Colendonk. Yonkers is so called after this Patroon. Patent issued for Kattskill. Breuckelen incorporated. Lake Saint Sacrament (now Lake George) discovered and explored by Father Jogues, S. J., who is afterwards murdered by the Mohawks. The land on which Philadelphia now stands, purchased by the Dutch.

1647. PETER STUYVESANT, Director. Estimated population of the Province 2,000. Church at New Amsterdam

ANNALS OF NEW NETHERLAND. XV

finished. Cornelis Melyn and Jochem Pietersen Kuyter, members of the former board of Eight men, prosecuted for opposing and complaining of the previous administration, heavily fined and banished. Shipwreck of the Princess, Ex-Director Kieft, Rev. Mr. Bogardus, Attorney General van der Huygens, and a number of others drowned. The Board of Nine Men appointed. Houses in New Amsterdam built of wood and thatched with straw. Influenza prevails throughout the country. Lady Stirling's agent arrested and sent to Holland. A Dutch ship seized at New Haven and brought to Manhattan.

1648. Fire Department and an Annual Fair established in New Amsterdam. Mission to Holland to represent the State of the Province proposed.

1649. General discontent. Papers of the Nine Men seized and Adriaen van der Donck, their President, imprisoned. Proceedings against Melyn and Kuyter disapproved in Holland, and they return to America in triumph. Delegates sent to Holland. Great Remonstrance of New Netherland presented to the States General. Kattskill and Claverack purchased for the Patroon of Renselaerswyck. Indian title to a large portion of the land in the present county of Westchester extinguished.

1650. Reforms in the Government and Institutions of New Netherland, reported by a committee of the States General, are opposed by the West India Company. Continued complaints by the Nine Men. Treaty concluded at Hartford determining the Boundary between the English and Dutch. Free navigation of the Hudson river declared.

1651. Continued arbitrary Government. Vice Director Van Dincklage expelled the Council for being opposed to Director Stuyvesant. Publications in Holland direct attention to New Netherland. Fort Casimir built at the Delaware.

1652. Beverwyck (Albany) separated from the Colonie of Rensselaerswyck and a distinct Court of Justice established there. Settlements begun at the Esopus, at Newtown and Flatbush, L. I. Nyack purchased and New Utrecht founded. Bibles first imported. Slaves to be imported direct from Africa. Population of New Amsterdam between seven and eight hundred souls. Municipal Government granted to that city. War between England and Holland. The Dutch send an embassy to Virginia to conclude a treaty with that Colony.

1653. Organization of a Municipal Government for New Amsterdam. Burgomasters and Schepens appointed. That city palisaded. Captain Underhill hoists the Parliament flag on Long Island, and is banished. Fort Good Hope on Connecticut river is seized by the English. Description of New Netherland prepared by Adriaen van der Donck. Rev. Mr. Drisius sent on an embassy to Virginia. Father Poncet, S. J., taken prisoner by the Mohawks, is sent back to Canada by way of Oswego. The Second Amboyna

Tragedy ; or a Faithful Account of a Bloody, Treacherous and Cruel Plot of the Dutch in America to murder the English Colonists, published in London. Convention of Delegates from several towns in New Netherland assemble at New Amsterdam, and vote a Remonstrance on the State of the Province, demanding a Representative form of government, &c., which is sent to the authorities in Holland. Oysterbay settled.

1654. Breuckelen granted additional privileges. Midwout and Amersfoort obtain the right to have local Magistrates. First Dutch Clergyman on Long Island appointed. Lutherans of New Amsterdam refused permission to call a minister. An Expedition against New Netherland sails from England. The English on Long Island disaffected. Peace with England concluded. General Thanksgiving. Salt Springs of Onondaga discovered. The Swedes surprise and seize Fort Casimir on the Delaware, and call it Fort Trinity. Emigrants from Connecticut settle in the town of Westchester.

1655. Flag of England raised at Gravesend, L. I. Swedes on the Delaware river reduced. Indians invade New Amsterdam and consequent collision. Hoboken, Pavonia and Staten Island laid waste. General consternation. First auction sale of Bibles, Psalm books, &c., in New Amsterdam.

1656. Orders issued to form compact villages. Proclamation issued against "Conventicles," or places of worship not in harmony with the Established Dutch Church. Westchester reduced under Dutch government, and Magistrates appointed for that Town. Rustdorp, or Jamico, L. I., planted. Hartford Treaty ratified by the States General. City of New Amsterdam surveyed. New Church built at Fort Orange, now Albany. Religious persecution revived. Baptist Minister of Flushing banished and Sheriff Hallett degraded for having harbored him. French settle on Lake Onondaga. Jesuit Missionaries among the Five Nations.

1657. Great and Small citizenship established in New Amsterdam. City of Amsterdam establishes a colonie called New Amstel, on the Delaware. Wreck of the ship Prince Maurice off Fire Island with a number of immigrants for that Colonie. Cromwell addresses a letter to the English on Long Island. Increased religious intolerance. Lutheran Minister banished. Quakers persecuted.

1658. Continued persecution of Quakers. Fines imposed on persons refusing to contribute to the support of the Dutch clergy. Flushing charter altered. Harlem founded as a place of amusement. Bergen (N. J.), purchased. Village of Communipa established. Trade opened by sea with Canada. French abandon their settlement at Onondaga. Village laid out at the Esopus.

1659. Massachusetts attempts to encroach on the Hudson river. Trade with France, Spain, Italy and the

Caribbean Islands permitted. Latin School established at New Amsterdam. War with the Esopus Indians. Delaware river claimed by Maryland. Dutch embassy to that Province.

1660. Haerlem incorporated. Peace concluded with the Esopus Indians. Clergymen appointed to Breuckelen and Esopus. Embassy to Virginia. Ambassador from Virginia arrives at New Amsterdam. Lord Baltimore renews his claim to the Delaware.

1661. Settlers invited to take up lands in what is now the State of New Jersey. Persecution of Quakers renewed. Wiltwyck, at Esopus, incorporated. Schenectady purchased. Bushwyck, New Utrecht and Bergen incorporated. Salt works erected on Coney Island.

1662. Encroachments of Connecticut; annexes Westchester and the English Towns on Long Island. Continued persecution of Quakers. John Bowne banished. New Proclamation against the public exercise of any religion but that of the Dutch Reformed Church.

1663. Religious persecution in New Netherland reproved by the authorities in Holland, and ceases in consequence. Puritans attempt a settlement at Raritan. An Earthquake in New Netherland. Small Pox commits great ravages. Massacre of Whites at the Esopus. War proclaimed against these Indians. The whole of the Delaware river surrendered to the City of Amsterdam. Connecticut ignores the existence of New Netherland. Convention of Dutch

Delegates at New Amsterdam. Names of the English villages on Long Island changed.

1664. New Netherland granted to the Duke of York. English Towns on Long Island elect Captain John Scott their President. General Provincial Assembly at New Amsterdam. Peace with the Esopus Indians. Schenectady surveyed and lots laid out. Connecticut claims the whole of Long Island. Population of the Province 10,000. New Netherland reduced by the English who give it the name of NEW YORK.

1673. New York recovered by the Dutch on the 9th of August, 1673, and the country from Maryland to Connecticut again called NEW NETHERLAND. New York city called New Orange; Albany, Willemstadt, and Kingston, Swanenburgh. September 19th, JACOB BENCKES appointed Governor.

1674. New Netherland ceded to the English in exchange for Surinam. On the 10th of November, New Orange is transferred to Major Edmund Andros, the English Governor, and that city and the Province are again called NEW YORK.

New Netherland Register.

DIRECTORS

OF THE AMSTERDAM CHAMBER OF THE WEST INDIA COMPANY WHO SUPERINTENDED THE AFFAIRS OF NEW NETHERLAND.

Extracted from the New York State Records.

1648. J. Specx,
   David van Baerle.
1649. Jacob Pergens,
   Joannes Ryckaert.
1650. Jacob Pergens,
   Jehan Raye,
   Ferdinand Schulenborch,
   Isaac van Beeck.

1651. A. Pater,
J. Specx,
David van Baerle,
F. Schulenborch,
Jacob Pergens,
Johan Le Thor,
Isaac van Beeck.
1652. David van Baerle,
Joannes Ryckaert,
Jacob Pergens,
Isaac van Beeck,
Ferdinand Schulenborch,
Eduard Man,
Paulus Timmerman.
1653. Eduard Man,
A. Pater,
Abr. Wilmerdonx,
David van Baerle,
Isaac van Beeck,
Joannes Ryckaert,
Jacob Pergens.
1654. Joannes Ryckaert,
Abr. Wilmerdonx,

Isaac van Beeck,
Eduard Man,
Paulus Timmerman,
David van Baerle.
1655. Hans Bontemantel,
Eduard Man,
Isaac van Beeck,
David van Baerle,
Jacob Pergens.
1656. David van Baerle,
Eduard Man,
Abr. Wilmerdonx,
Isaac van Beeck,
Paulus Timmerman,
Hans Bontemantel.
1657. Isaac van Beeck,
Abr. Wilmerdonx.
Eduard Man,
C. Witsen.
1658. Hans Bontemantel,
Abr. Wilmerdonx,
David van Baerle,
C. Witsen.

1659. Abr. Wilmerdonx,
Paulus Timmerman,
Jacob Pergens,
Joannes Ryckaert,
Hans Bontemantel,
Eduard Man,
David van Baerle.
1660. David van Bacrle,
Eduard Man,
C. Witsen,
Abr. Wilmerdonx,
Coenraet Burgh,
Jacob Pergens.
1661. Hans Bontemantel,
Jacob Pergens,
David van Baerle,
Abr. Wilmerdonx,
Coenraet Burgh,
C. Witsen,
Eduard Man,
Jacobus Reynst.
1662. Hans Bontemantel,
David van Baerle,

Jacob Pergens,
Abr. Wilmerdonx.
1663. David van Baerle,
Hans Bontemantel,
Abr. Wilmerdonx,
Dirck Spiegel,
Jacobus Reynst.
1664. Abr. Wilmerdonx,
Cornelis Clerk,
Dirck Spiegel,
Hans Bontemantel,
David van Baerle.

COMMISSIONERS

OF NEW AMSTEL, OR THE COLONIE OF THE CITY OF AMSTERDAM, ON THE DELAWARE RIVER.

1658. Cornelis De Graeff,
Nicolaes van Loon,
Cornelis Geelvinck.

1659. Cornelis De Graeff,
Nicolas Tulp,
Gilles Valckenier,
Henrick Hooft,
Peter Cloeck,
Coenradt Burgh.

1661. Coenradt Burgh,
Hendrick Roeters,
Eduard Man,
Johannes Tayspil,
Anthony Casteleyn.

1662. Coenradt Burgh,
Hendrick Roeters,
Johannes Tayspil.

PATROONS OF NEW NETHERLAND.

Pavonia.

1630. Michael Paauw, Lord of Achtien-hoven.
Surrendered in 1636 or 1637.

Swanendael.

1630–31. Samuel Godyn and Samuel Blommaert.
Surrendered 7th February, 1635.

Rensselaerswyck.

1631. Kiliaen van Rensselaer.

Achter Col to *Tapaan.*

1641. Meyndert Meyndertsen van Keren, Lord of Nederhorst.

Staten Island.

1642.   Cornelis Melyn.

Surrendered 14 June, 1659.

Colendonck.

1646.   Adriaen van der Donck.

One-third of Staten Island.

1650.   Hendrick van der Capelle, Lord of Ryssel.

Surrendered 20 November, 1660.

Nevesinck and *Tapaan.*

1651.   Cornelis van Werckhoven.

He afterwards abandoned these, and in 1652 established a colonie at Nyack, *hodie* New Utrecht, L. I.

South River or *Delaware.*

1656.   City of Amsterdam.

DIRECTORS GENERAL.

1623.	Adriaen Joris.
1624.	Cornelis Jacobsen Mey.
1625.	William Verhulst.
1626 May 4.	Peter Minuit.
1632 March.	*The Council.*
1633 April.	Wouter van Twiller.
1638 Mar. 28.	William Kieft. Commission issued September, 1637.
1647 May 11.	Peter Stuyvesant. Commission issued 28th July, 1646.
1650 Sept. 17.	*The Council;* Stuyvesant at Hartford.
1650 Oct. 12.	Peter Stuyvesant.*
1654 Dec. 24.	*The Council;* Stuyvesant at the West Indies.

---

* In July, 1651, the Director General went to the South River; the government was administered in his absence until August by the Council.

1655 July 11.   Peter Stuyvesant.*
1663 Sept. 7.   The Council; Stuyvesant at Boston.
1663 Oct. 9.   Peter Stuyvesant.

1664 Sept. 6.   New Netherland usurped by the English.

New Netherland retaken by the Dutch.
1673 Aug. 12.   Cornelis Everts, jr., Jacob Benckes, and Council of War.
1673 Sept. 19. Jacob Benckes.

* August 31, 1655, and April 20, 1658, the Director General went again to the South River, and the government devolved on the Council during his brief absence.

COUNCIL.

This body acted in a twofold capacity; as an Executive Council and as a Court of Justice. The Members could not be sued before, and were not amenable to, a Court of inferior jurisdiction. On extraordinary occasions, it was usual to adjoin some of the Inhabitants or Public Servants to the Board, and the Captains of the Company's ships, when on shore, had a voice therein. The Schout-fiscal had a seat, but no vote, in the Council; when he acted as prosecuting officer he retired from the Bench.

1626.

Isaac de Rasieres,
Peter Bylvelt,
Jacob Elbertsen Wissinck,
Jan Jansen Brouwer,
Symon Dircksen Pos,
Reynert Harmensen,
Jan Lampo, *Schout-fiscal.*

1630.

Peter Bylvelt,
Reynert Harmensen,
Jan Jansen Myndertsen,

Jacob Elbertsen Wissinck,
Jan Jansen Brouwer,
Symon Dircksen Pos,*
Jan Lampo, *Schout-fiscal.*

1633.

Jacob Jansen Hesse,
Martin Gerritsen (van Bergen),
Andries Hudde,
Jacques Bentyn,
Lubertus van Dincklage, *Schout-fiscal.*

1636.

Andries Hudde,
Claes van Elslant,
Jacobus van Curler,
Jacques Bentyn, *Schout-fiscal.*

1637.

Andries Hudde,
Claes van Elslant,

---

* Went to Rensselaerswyck in 1630, and died 1649.

Jacobus van Curler,
Jacques Bentyn, *Schout-fiscal.**

1638.

Mar. 28. Johannes La Montagne,
Ulrich Lupold, *Schout-fiscal.*

1639.

Johannes La Montagne,
Ulrich Lupold,
July 13. Corn. van der Huyghens, *Schout-fiscal.*

1642.

Johannes La Montagne,
Corn. van der Huyghens, *Schout-fiscal.*
Nov. 18. Jacques Bentyn,†
Jochim Pietersen Kuyter,
Hendrick van Dyck,
Gysbert op Dyck.

---

* Returned to Holland about 1648.

† These four were adjoined to Mr. La Montagne, pro hac vice, for the trial of one Hendrick Jansen, for having slandered the Director General.

1643.

Johannes La Montagne,
Corn. van der Huyghens, *Schout-fiscal.*

1644.

Johannes La Montagne,
Corn. van der Huyghens, *Schout-fiscal.*
July 14. Bastiaen Jansen Krol,*
Willem Cornelissen Oldemarckt,
Jan de Fries,
Hendrick van Dyck.

1645.

Johannes La Montagne,
Corn. van der Huyghens, *Schout-fiscal.*
April 28. Johan de Fries,†
Gysbert de Leeuw,
Oloff Stevensen van Cortland,

---

* These four were adjoined, pro hac vice, to try a case in which the defendant objected to the Director General and Councillor La Montagne.

† These seven were adjoined, pro hac vice, to consider measures against the Indians.

Gysbert op Dyck.
May 24. John Underhill,
Jan Evertsen Bout,
Jacob Stoffelsen.

1646.

Johannes La Montagne,
Corn. van der Huyghens, *Schout-fiscal.*

1647.

May 11. William Kieft, *Ex-Director*,*
Lubertus van Dincklage,†
Johannes La Montagne,
Brian Newton,‡

---

* Left the country, 16 August.

† Vice-director; presided in the Council when it sat as a Court of Justice.

‡ Entered the Company's service in 1630, and served afterwards in different places, lastly at Curaçao under Stuyvesant, with whom he came to New Netherland as captain-lieutenant, which office he resigned July, 1654. He had already been removed from the office of commissary in June, and went to live to Amersfoort. He went to Holland same year, and returned to this country February, 1655, having been restored to his military position.

Paulus Leendertsen van der Grist, *Naval-officer.*
Jacob Loper, *Commander,*
Jelmer Thomassen, *Captain of the Great Gerrit.**
Jan Claessen Bol, *Captain of the Princess*†
Hendrick van Dyck, *Schout-fiscal.*‡
Sept. 20. Adriaen Keyser, *Commissary.*

1648.

Lubertus van Dincklage,
Johannes La Montagne,

---

* Ordered to the West Indies, 28 June.

† Sailed from New Netherland, 16 August.

‡ Had previously served as Ensign, under Director Kieft, against the Indians; was commissioned *fiscal* 28 June, 1645. In New Netherland, he was admitted to a seat in the Council at the mere pleasure of the Director Stuyvesant, who, he says, excluded him twenty-nine months from the court. Van der Donck makes the same statement. It would seem, however, that he was excluded only twenty months in New Netherland. He held the office until 27 March, 1652, when he was dismissed.

Brian Newton,
Paulus Leendertsen van der Grist,
Adriaen Keyser.

1649.

Lubertus van Dincklage,
Johannes La Montagne,
Brian Newton,
Paulus Leendertsen van der Grist,
Adriaen Keyser.
Jan. 2. Hendrick van Dyck, *Schout-fiscal.*

1650.

Lubertus van Dincklage,*
Johannes La Montagne,
Brian Newton,

---

* Was forcibly thrust from and expelled the Council by order of Director Stuyvesant, 28 Feb., 1651; but so high was his character as a jurist and a man, that orders were sent from Holland the same year for his reinstatement. Before these were received, Mr. van D. had removed to Staten Island, where he acted as agent for Mr. Van der Capelle. He is mentioned as deceased in 1658, when the Rev. Joannes Hanius, who married Margareta van Dincklage, applied as heir at law, for a settlement of the estate.

Adriaen Keyser,
Hendrick van Dyck, *Schout-fiscal.*

1651.

Lubertus van Dincklage,
Johannes La Montagne,
Brian Newton,
Adriaen Keyser,
Hendrick van Dyck, *Schout-fiscal.*

1652.

Johannes La Montagne,
Brian Newton.
March. Cornelis van Tienhoven, *Schout-fiscal.*

1653.

Johannes La Montagne,
Brian Newton,
Cornelis van Tienhoven, *Schout-fiscal.*
May. Cornelis van Werkhoven.
Oct. Nicasius de Sille, *First Councillor.*
Commission dated 24 July.

Dec. 16. Cornelis Coenraatsen, *Commander of the ship King Solomon.*

1654.

Nicasius de Sille,
Johannes La Montagne,
Cornelis van Werckhoven,*
Cornelis van Tienhoven, *Schout-fiscal.*

1655.

Nicasius de Sille,
Johannes La Montagne,
Cornelis van Tienhoven, *Schout-fiscal.*
Aug. 31. Allard Anthony,
Martin Cregier, *Burgomasters.*†

1656.

Nicasius de Sille,

---

* Came from Utrecht; appears in the Council for the last time 14 Sept., 1654, in which year he returned to Holland, where he died in 1655. He was the founder of New Utrecht, on Long Island.

† Adjoined to the Council pending the absence of the Director General and Mr. de Sille at the South River.

Johannes La Montagne,*
Cornelis van Tienhoven, *Schout-fiscal*,
 Dismissed 7 June.
June 20. Nicasius de Sille, *Schout-fiscal*,
Cornelis van Ruyven, *Secretary*.†

1657.

Nicasius de Sille, *Schout-fiscal*.
Jan. 3. Peter Tonneman.

1658.

Nicasius de Sille, *Schout-fiscal*,
Peter Tonneman.
Mar. 19. Johannes de Decker, *Comptroller*.
 Commission dated 20 December, 1657.

1659.

Nicasius de Sille, *Schout-fiscal*,

---

* Appointed Vice-director at Fort Orange, 28th September, 1656.

† Was invited to vote, pro hac vice, on a case in appeal, the Council being equally divided.

| | Peter Tonneman,*
Johannes de Decker.† |
|---|---|
| Feb. 10. | Cornelis van Ruyven, *Receiver-general.* |
| | With an advisory and concluding vote on all questions of Finance. |

1660.

	Nicasius de Sille, *Schout-fiscal.*
Mar. 15.	Cornelis van Ruyven,‡
	Martin Cregier,
	Oloff Stevensen van Cortland.
Aug. 5.	Johannes de Decker.

1661.

	Nicasius de Sille, *Schout-fiscal,*
	Johannes de Decker.
Dec.	Cornelis van Ruyven, *Receiver-general.*

---

* Went to Holland in the fall of this year.

† Absent from the country from 29 July, 1659, to 12 July, 1660.

‡ These three were adjoined to the Council in the absence of the Director-General at Esopus, and of Mr. de Sille at the South River.

1662.

Nicasius de Sille, *Schout-fiscal,*
Johannes de Decker,
Cornelis van Ruyven, *Receiver-general.*

1663.

Nicasius de Sille, *Schout-fiscal,*
Johannes de Decker,
Cornelis van Ruyven, *Receiver-general.*

1664.

Nicasius de Sille, *Schout-fiscal,*
Johannes de Decker,
Cornelis van Ruyven, *Receiver-general.*

Sept. *Province usurped by the English.*

1673.

New Netherland retaken by the Dutch.

Aug. 12. Commander Cornelis Evertse,
Commander Jacob Benkes,

Captain Anthony Colve,
Captain Nicolaes Boes,
Captain Abraham van Zyll.
Sept. 19. Cornelis Steenwick.
Dec. 15. William Knyff, *Schout-fiscal.*

1674.

Cornelis Steenwyck,
William Knyff, *Schout-fiscal.*
Feb. 1. Cornelis van Ruyven, *adjoined.*
Feb. 15. Nicolas Bayard, *adjoined.*

COMMANDER

OF THE COMPANY'S SHIPS IN THE ABSENCE OF THE DIRECTOR-GENERAL.

1647 May 27. Jelmer Thomas.

NAVAL OFFICER,

OR, SUPERINTENDENT OF NAVAL EQUIPMENTS.

1647 May 27. Paul Leendertsen van der Grist.

PRESIDENT

OF THE INFERIOR COURT, NEW AMSTERDAM.

16—.   The Director General.
1647 July 22.   Lubertus van Dincklage.
1654.   A Burgomaster, or
                The Schout-fiscal.

RECEIVERS GENERAL.

1644 Aug. 4.   William de Key; dead 1658.
1647 Mar. 11. Roelof Jansen de Haes.
1649 Aug.   Cornelis van Tienhoven,
1652   Adriaen van Tienhoven.
               Dismissed March 1656, and absconded.
1656 June.   Cornelis van Ruyven,
               Also Treasurer and Keeper of the Books of Finance.

1673 Sept. 20. Nicolas Bayard.

COMPTROLLER.

1657 Dec. 20. Johannes de Decker.
Sworn 19th March, 1658.

COMPTROLLER OF WINDMILL.

Johannes Provoost.
1656 Sept. 27. William Bogardus.

BOARD OF AUDIT.

1658 May 25. Director General and
Two of the Council, whereof
Receiver General shall be one.

COMMISSARIES OF ACCOUNTS,
or Book-keepers.

Isaac de Rasières.
1633.   Cornelis van Tienhoven.
1647 May.   Adriaen Keyser,
To March 20, 1653.

1651 April 26. Johannes Dyckman,*
                Carel van Brugge.
1653 Mar. 20. Johannes La Montagne, junr.,
                vice Keyser.
1659 Mar. 31. Jacob Sam,† *vice* Van Brugge,
                dismissed.
1663 July 23. Jan Adriaensz van Duyvelant,
                vice Sam returned to Holland.

1674 Mar. 24. Jacobus van de Water.

Clerks in Book-keeper's Office.

                Vincent Pickes,
                Johannes La Montagne, junr.
1655 Feb. 21. Matthys Capito.
1655 June 20. Martin Cregier, junr.

---

* Had been First Clerk to the Chamber at Amsterdam, and sailed from Holland in April, 1651; went to Fort Orange, as Commissary, in the same year.

† Had been appointed in Holland on this date, and came over with his family; arrived at the Manhattans in July.

1657 Mar. 27. Matthys Capito, *Assistant Commissary of Accounts.**

1658 June 20. Martin Cregier, junr., *de novo.*

PROVINCIAL SECRETARIES.

1626 July 27. Isaac de Rasières.
1628. Jan van Remund.
163–. Andries Hudde.
1638 April 1. Cornelis van Tienhoven.
1649. Adriaen Keyser.
1650. Jacob Kip, *acting.*
1651 April. Cornelis van Tienhoven, Reappointed in Holland.
1652. Carel van Brugge.†
1653 Nov. Cornelis van Ruyven.

1673 Aug. 20. Nicolas Bayard.

---

* Was sent in 1660 to the Delaware, to make out a correct account of the estate of the late Vice Director Arichs. Removed finally to the Esopus.

† Died at Flushing, L. I., in 1682.

English Secretaries.

1642 Dec. 11. George Baxter.
1647 June 28, George Baxter.
1654.   Carel van Brugge.
1657 July 1.   Nicolas Bayard.

Deputy Secretaries.

1628.   Lanaert Cole.
1650.   Jacob Hendricksen Kip.

Clerks in Secretary's Office.

1643.   William de Key.
1646.   Martin Cregier, jun.
   Resigned 16th May, 1661.
  Johannes Rodenberch.
1647.   Adriaen van Tienhoven,
  Jacob Hendricksen Kip.
1651   Andries Johannes Christman.
   Returned to Holland 8th April, 1651.

NEW NETHERLAND REGISTER.

1653.		Levinus van Ruyven.*
1654.		Balthazar Bayard; left in 1660, Nicholas Bayard.
	Sept. 8.	Jan Lubbertsen.
1655	Oct.	William Bogardus, First Clerk in 1663.
1657	Jan.	Laurence de Sille, Resigned 17th May, 1663.
1658	May 25.	Jan Adriaensz van Duyvelant, To April, 1663.
	July 11.	Hendrick van der Walle.
1659	Mar. 17.	Dirck Looten; left in 1661.
1660.		Peter van Ruyven.

1673.		Abram Varlett, Ephraim Herman.

---

* June 28, 1653, had a free passage to New Netherland on condition that he should serve six months in the Secretary's office without pay; went in 1655 to Curaçao, of which Island he became Secretary.

COMMISSARIES OF STORES.

1628.	Jan Huyghen.
	Dirck Corssen,
	Maurits Jansen.
1633.	Claes van Elslant, *of Provisions*,
	Jacob Stoffelsen,
	Jacobus van Corlear, *of Wares* or *Cargoes; vice* Corssen.
1637.	Andries Hudde, *of Wares*.
1638 April 7.	Jan Willemsen Schut, *Assistant*, Wybrant Pietersen, *of Wares*.
1639 July 21.	Ulrich Lupold,* *vice* Pietersen, Laurens Haen, *Assist. to Lupold;* Dismissed in 1641.
1640 Jan. 5.	David Provoost, *of Provisions; vice* Elsland resigned.
July 1.	Oloff Stevensen van Cortland, *vice* Corlear.

---

* Lupold was guilty of malversation in March 1641, and dismissed, but on petition and promise of amendment, some respectable Englishmen having interceded in his behalf, he was restored.

NEW NETHERLAND REGISTER. 31

1640 Aug. 23. Maurits Jansen, *vice* Provoost dismissed.
   Harmen van de Bogaert.
1642. Gysbert Opdyck, *of Provisions*,
   Evert Duyckinck, *Assistant.*
1643. David Provoost,
   Peter Anthony, *Assistant,*
   Adriaen Dircksen, *Assistant,*
   Adam Roelantsen, *Weighmaster.*
1646. Laurens van Heusden.
1647. Jesse La Montagne,
   Adriaen van Tienhoven, *of Imports and Exports.**
1648 Sept. 4. Matthys Capito, *Assistant ; vice* Anthony.
   Hendrick Eldersen.

---

* The Commissary of Imports and Exports was an officer of the customs, whose duty it was to take care that all imported goods were conveyed to the public store, and delivered to the right owners, according to their invoices, and that all goods for export to Holland be sent to the store to be marked with the Company's mark. He was to keep a proper record of all cases and packages, and also of their marks, from whom received, and to whom consigned.

1648. Brian Newton.
1653. Carel van Brugge, *of Provisions, Liquors and Munitions of War.*
Johannes Provoost, *Assistant,* Went to Fort Orange in 1656.
1655. Foppe Jansen, to the South river expedition.
1657 April 7. Nicolas Varlet, *of Imports and Exports, vice* Tienhoven.
April 16. Warnaer Wessels, *Searcher, Inspector and Guager.*
1658. Nicolas Varlet, *Searcher and Inspector, vice* Wessels dismissed.*
1659 Dec. 30. Jacob Sam, *of Imports and Exports.*
1661 Jan. 20. Carel van Brugge, *vice* Sam.
Mar. 28. Dirck Looten, *vice* Van Brugge.
1662 Dec. 28. Jacob Sam, reappointed.

---

* He was dismissed in consequence of becoming Farmer of the Revenue, which no officer of the Company was allowed to do.

1663 Aug. 16. Nicholas Bayard, *of Imports and Exports*, vice Sam returned to Holland.

Sept. 27. Gerrit Kocx, South river.

FARMERS OF THE REVENUE.

In 1655, the authorities in Holland recommended that certain sources of revenue in New Netherland be farmed.

1654 Dec. 1. Warnaer Wessels, of *Excise*, New Amsterdam, Brueckelen, Midwout and Amesfoort.

1655. Dec. 1. Isaac de Foreest, of the *Weighhouse.*

Warnaer Wessels, of *Excise*, New Amsterdam and the Dutch towns on Long Island.

1655 May 1. Marcelis Jansen, of *Excise*, Fort Orange.

1656. Paulus van der Beeck, of *Duties on furs and liquors exported to places other than Holland*, and *Citizens' Excise*, New Amsterdam.

1656 April 8. Isaac de Foreest, of the *Weighhouse.*

Nov. 30. Warnaer Wessels, of *Tavern Excise*, New Amsterdam.

Sept. Solomon La Chair, of *Slaughter Excise.*

1656. Harmen Jacobsen Bamboes, of *Excise*, Fort Orange.

1657. Gerrit Hendricks, of *Slaughter Excise.*

Nov. 30. Warnaer Wessels, of *Tavern Excise*, New Amsterdam.

Jan La Montagne, of *Tavern Excise*, New Amsterdam and Long Island.

Henrick Bierman, of *Excise*, Fort Orange.

Warnaer Wessels, of *Duties on peltries, wine and beer exported to places other than Holland.*

1658. Jan La Montagne, of *Tavern Excise*, Long Island.

Mar. 26. Richard Brudenell, *Deputy Collector of Excise*, Hempstead.

1658	Marcelis Jansen, of *Excise*, Fort Orange.
	Warnaer Wessels, of the *Weighhouse*.
	Adriaen Jansen from Leyden, alias Appel, of *Excise*, Fort Orange.
April 23.	Nicolas Varlet, of *Duties on Exports and Imports* to and from New England and Virginia.
1659.	Warnaer Wessels, of the *Weighhouse*.
1660 May 6.	Nicolas Varlet, of *Duties on Exports and Imports* to and from New England and Virginia.
	Isaac de Foreest, of *Tavern Excise*.
	Solomon La Chair, of *Excise*, Long Island.
1661 April 11.	Gerrit Hendricksen van Harderwyck, of the *Weigh-house*.
	Warnaer Wessels, of *Tavern Excise*, New Amsterdam.*

---

* Became a defaulter in 1662.

1661		Edward Hart, *Collector* at Flushing.
	June 2.	Paulus van der Beeck, of *Excise*, Long Island.
	July 6.	Warnaer Wessels, and Paulus van der Beecq, of *Tenths*.
	Oct.	Jan Gerritsen van Marcken, of *Tavern Excise*, Fort Orange.
1662.		Roeloff Jansen, Collector of *Excise*, Flushing.
	Mar. 23.	Gerrit Hendricksen van Harderwyck, of the *Weigh-house*.
		Jonas Bartels, of *Tavern Excise*.
		Warnaer Wessels, and Gerrit Hendricks, of *Duties on peltries, wine, brandy, and other liquors exported to the North*.
	Nov.	Jan Gerritsen van Marcken, of *Tavern Excise*, Fort Orange.
1663.		Jonas Bartels, of *Excise*, New Amsterdam.

1663.		Otto Gerrits, of *Slaughter Excise*.
	April 19.	Gerrit Hendricksen van Harderwyck, of the *Weigh-house*.
	Oct.	William Bout, of *Excise*, Fort Orange.

SURVEYORS GENERAL.

1642 June 19. Andries Hudde.
1648. Claes van Elslant.
1654 Dec. 17. Andries Hudde.
1655. Peter W. van Couwenhoven, Claes van Elslant.
1657 Jan. 23. Jacques Corteljou.

1673. Walter Wharton, *Delaware*.

PROVINCIAL SCHOUT-FISCALS.

This officer discharged the duties of Attorney General and Sheriff; in the latter capacity he was allowed Deputies, who attended to levying executions, &c.

1626.		Jan Lampo.
1632.		Coenraad Notelman.
1633.		Lubertus van Dincklage.
1636.		Jacques Bentyn.
1638	Mar. 28.	Ulrich Lupold.*
1639	July 13.	Cornelis van der Huyghens.†
1647	May 22.	Hendrick van Dyck.

Commission dated 28th June, 1645.

1652 Mar. 27. Cornelis van Tienhoven.

Dismissed 7th June, 1656.

1656 June 26. Nicasius de Sille.

1673 Dec. 15. William Knyff.

---

* Was from Staden in Bremen. His wife's name was Petronella Underhil. He was appointed Fiscal in Holland in 1637, but arrived in New Netherland this year.

† Drowned in the voyage to Holland 27th Sept., 1647.

Deputy Provincial Schout-Fiscals.

1638. William Bredenbent.
1658 May 25. Resolved Waldron.
Aug. 13. Nicolas Albrechts,
Hendrick Muller.
1661 Mar. 3. Hans Vos.

Local Schout-Fiscals.

Fort Orange.

Vice Director, *ex officio.*

Deputies.

1656. Jan Daniels.
1658. Jacob Teunissen.
Dismissed in August for selling liquor to Indians.
1658. Hans Vosch.

Rensselaerswyck.

1630. Jacob Albertsen Planck.
1641. Adriaen van der Donck.

1645.   Nicolas Coorn.
1646 Mar. 22. Gerrit van Slechtenhorst.
       May   Brant Arent van Slechtenhorst.
1650.   Cornelis Teunissen.
1652 April 24. Gerrit Swart.

Willemstadt and Rensselaerswsyck.
1673 Oct. 6. Andrew Draeyer.

Schanegtede.
1673 Sept. 18. Jan Gerritsen van Marcken.

Esopus.
1661 May 23. Roeloff Swartwout.
1663 Dec. 19. Matthys Capito.
1664 Feb. 14. Roeloff Swartwout.
       July 4. William Beeckman.

1673 Oct. 30. Isaac Grevenraet.

New Amsterdam.

1661, Feb. 1. Ordered, that the City Sheriff shall preside at the meeting of Burgomasters and Schepens, and have a voice and vote in the nomination of Magistrates, and in all matters wherein he is not a party.

Schout-fiscal of New Netherland, until 1660.

1654 May 18. Jochem Pietersen Kuyter,
Murdered by Indians before the receipt of his commission.

July 21. Jacques Corteljou,
Declined the appointment.

1660 April 9. Peter Tonneman,
Sworn 5th August.

New Orange.

1673 Sept. 8. Anthony de Milt.
Died in 1689.

Haerlem.

1661. Johannes La Montagne, juni.
1673. Resolved Waldron.

Westchester.

1654. Thomas Wheeler.

Breuckelen District.

1646.	Jan Teunissen.
1654.	David Provoost.*
1656 Jan. 25.	Peter Tonneman, *vice* Provoost deceased.
1659.	Peter Hegeman, *Acting*, in the absence of Tonneman in Holland.
1660 June 25.	Peter Hegeman, *vice* Tonneman appointed to New Amsterdam†
1661.	Adriaen Hegeman.‡

1673 Aug. 18. Jacob Stryker.§

---

* Midwout and Amersfoort included in this Bailiwick.

† On the appointment of Tonneman to New Amsterdam, the Directors in Holland, 16th April, 1660, offered the Sheriffalty of Breuckelen to Resolved Waldron. But their wishes were not carried out, "as he was not a good penman."

‡ Boswyck and New Utrecht annexed to the Breuckelen district, which was thenceforth called, *The Five Dutch Towns.*

§ Gravesend annexed to the district, which now constitutes Kings county.

New Utrecht.

1660 Feb. 23. Nicasius de Sille, or his Deputy.
Annexed to Breuckelen in 1661.

Boswyck.

1661. Senior Magistrate, *ex officio*.
Afterwards annexed to Breuckelen.

Gravesend.

1650. James Hubbard.
1651. Richard Gibbons.
1653 March. John Morris.
Died 1657.
1656 Mar. 25. John Cooke.
1657 Mar. 27. Charles Morgan.
Was appointed annually down to 1663.
1673. Town annexed to the Breuckelen district.

Middleburgh.

1653. Thomas Newton.
1654. Elias Bayley.
1660. Mar. 9. Thomas Pettit.
Elias Bayley would serve notwithstanding, although "not a vote was cast for him."

Flushing.

Jamaica and Hempstead were included, I think, in this district.

1647. William Harck.
Died 1658.

1648 April 27. John Underhill, *vice* Harck dismissed for having married a couple. In May, 1653, Sheriff Underhill threw off the Dutch yoke in a long Vindication, and it is probable that, in consequence of the war between Holland and England, no successor was appointed, until

1655 April 22. John Hicks.

1656 Mar. 25. William Hallet,
Removed 8th Nov. for having permitted a Baptist minister to officiate in his house, and for having received the Last Supper at his hands.

1657. Tobias Feake,
Dismissed January 1658, for sympathizing with Quakers.

1658 Mar. 26. Presiding Magistrate, *ex officio.*
John Mastine, *Town Constable.*

Flushing, Hempstead, Rustdorp, Middelburgh and Oysterbay, or, The Five English Towns.

1673 Aug. 31. William Lawrence.
1674 Mar. 24. Francis Bloodgood,
   Chief officer of the Dutch residents of Flushing, Hempstead, Jamaica and Newtown.

Southampton, Seatalcot, Huntington, Easthamtpon, and Southold.

1673 Sept. 8. Isaac Arnold.
   Forced by the people to resign.

Huntington and Seatalcot.

1673 Nov. 21. Presiding Magistrate, *ex officio.*

Staten Island.

1673 Aug. 25. Peter Biljou.

*Achter Col.**

1673 Sept. 1. John Ogden.

---

* Comprised Elizabethtown, Woodbridge, Shrewsbury, Newark, Piscattaway and Middletown, now in New Jersey.

Bergen.*

1661 Aug. 4. Tielman van Vleeck.
1673 Aug. 18. Claes Arentse Stoers.

Fort Casimir (Delaware).

1656 Jan. 4. Andries Hudde.

New Amstel (Delaware).

1657 Aug. 10. Andries Hudde.
1659.   Gerrit van Sweringen.
> Suspended Aug. 1662, for having committed a homicide; reinstated 1st May, 1663.

Swedish Settlement on the Delaware.

1656.   Gregorius van Dyck.
1661 Mar. 21. William Beeckman, *ex officio*.

Altona (Delaware).

1658 July.   Vice Director, *ex officio*.
1658.   Matthýs Bengson, *Deputy*,
> Died 9th Sept., 1662.

1662 Sept. 28. Jan Daniels, *Deputy*. (See *Fort Orange*.)

---

* Originally called, The New Village in the Maizeland.

South River, or *Delaware*.*
1673 Sept. 19. Peter Alrighs.

COMMISSARIES OF DISTRICTS.

Fort Nassau (North River).

1614.	Hendrick Christiaensen.
	Jacob Eelkins, *Factor*.

Fort Orange.

1623.	Daniel Krieckenbeeck,
	Murdered by Indians, 1626.
1626.	Peter Barentsen.
	Bastiaen Jansen Krol.
	Dirck Cornelissen Duyster, *Deputy*.
1633.	Hans Jorissen Houten.
1638 July 15.	Adriaen Dircksen, *Assistant*.†
1640.	Jean Labadie, *Assistant*.
1641.	Bastiaen Jansen Crol.

---

* Included New Amstel, Upland and Whorekil.

† Because he speaks correctly the Mohawk language, and is well versed in the art of trading with these Indians.

1645.   Harmen Myndertsz van den Bogart.*
1647 Nov. 6. Carel van Brugge.
1651.   Johannes Dyckman.
1655 June 21. Johannes de Decker, *President of the Court and Commissary.*
1656 Sept. 28. Johannes La Montagne, *Vice Director and Sheriff.*
Entered on his duties 4th October.

Called *Fort Nassau* in 1673.

1673 Oct. 6. Andries Drayer.

Esopus.

1658 June 24. Andries Lourentsen, *Commander*,
Oct. 18. Dirck Smith, *Commander.*
1663.   Ensign Niessen, *Commander.*
1664 July 4. William Beeckman.

---

* Was born in 1612, and came to New Netherland 24th May, 1630, as Surgeon of the Eendraght, in which capacity he served until 1633. He made a voyage to the West Indies in 1638, and met an untimely end in 1647 or 1648, having been burned to death in an Indian wigwam on the Mohawk River. His widow married Jean Labadie.

NEW NETHERLAND REGISTER.

Pavonia.

1633.	Michel Paulusz, *Commander*.
1636.	Cornelis van Voorst.

Fort Good Hope (Connecticut).

1633. Jacobus van Corlear.
1638. Gysbert Opdyck.
1640 Oct. 25. Jan Hendrick Roesen.*
1641 June 6. Johannes La Montagne.†
1642 April. David Provoost.
1647 June 20. Gysbert Opdyck.

Fort Nassau (Delaware River).

1633. Arendt Corssen.
1838. Jan Jansen van Ilpendam,
   Dead 1647.
1645 Oct. 12. Andries Hudde.
1647 Sept. 20. Andries Hudde,
   Alexander Boyer, *Assistant*.

---

* Died shortly after arriving at his post.
† Was sent thither with a force of fifty soldiers to defend the Fort against the aggressions of the English.

Fort Casimir.

1652.	Gerrit Bicker.
	Surrendered it to the Swedes.
1655 Sept.	Dirck Smith, *Provisional com'der.*
1655 Nov. 29.	Jean Paul Jacquet, *Vice Director and Commander-in-Chief.*
	Sworn 3d Dec. 1655; removed 20th April 1657.
1657 April 20.	Andries Hudde,
	Jan Juriaensen Becker,
	Paulus Jansen, *Commissioners to manage the affairs of the Fort.*

New Amstel (late Fort Casimir).

1657 April 21. Jacob Alrichs.
1659 Dec. 30. Alexander d'Hinojossa.

Swedish Settlement.

1656.   Hendrick Huyghens, *Commis'ry.*

Tinnccum.

1662.   Joost de la Grange, *Councillor.*

Altona.

1657 April.   Andries Hudde,

Paulus Jansen,
Jan Juriaensen Becker, *Commissioners.*

1658 July 30. William Beeckman,

Whorekil.

1660 Jan. Peter Alrichs, *Commander.**

COUNCIL.

Fort Casimir and New Amstel.

1655 Dec. 18. Andries Hudde,
Elmerhuysen Kleyn,
Gysbert Braey,
Hans Hopman,
Returned to Holland, 1657.

1656 Sept. Paulus Jansen, *vice* Hopman.

1657. Alexander d'Hinojossa,
Abraham Rynevelt, *Storekeeper,*
Cornelis van Gezel, *Storekeeper.*

1659 Nov. 26. Gerrit van Sweringen, *vice* Rynevelt, deceased.

---

* Had been Commissary at New Amstel in 1656, 7.

1660 Jan.   Jan Crato, *vice* Gezel removed.
　　　　　　　Elmerhuysen Kleyn,
　　　　　　　　Died 1661.
　　　　　　　Jan Willemsen,
　　　　　　　　Died November, 1662.
1661.   Peter Petersen Herder.
1663 Dec. 3. Peter Alrichs,
　　　　　　　Israel Alrichs,
　　　　　　　Henry Cousturier.

REPRESENTATIVES OF THE COMMONALTY.

The Twelve Men.

This Board represented Manhattan, Breuckelen and Pavonia, and were elected to suggest means to punish the Indians for a murder they had committed. This is the first glimmer of a Representative form of Government within the limits of the present States of New York and New Jersey.

1641 Aug. 29. David Pietersen de Vries, *President*,
　　　　　　　Jacques Bentyn,
　　　　　　　Jan Jansen Dam,
　　　　　　　　Dead 1651.

Hendrick Jansen,*
Maryn Adriaensen,
Abram Pietersen, the *Miller*.
Fredrick Lubbertsen,
Jochim Pietersen Kuyter,
Gerrit Dircksen,
George Rapalje,
Abram Planck,
Jacob Stoffelsen.

In a subsequent record occur the names of:

John Evertsen Bout,
Jacob Walingen.

1642 Feb. 18. Board abolished.

The Eight Men.

Elected to adopt measures against the Indians. These delegates were to meet every Saturday for deliberation. Five was a quorum.

1643 Sept. 13. Jochim Pietersen Kuyter,

---

* Banished in November 1642, for having spoken disrespectfully of Governor Kieft.

Jan Jansen Dam,
Barent Dircksen,
Abraham Pietersen, the *Miller*.
Isaac Allerton,
Thomas Hall,
Gerrit Wolphertsen (van Couwenhoven),
Cornelis Melyn.

Sept. 15. Jan Evertsen Bout, *vice* Dam expelled.

1645.
Jacob Stoffelsen,
John Underhill,
Francis Douty,
George Baxter,
Richard Smith,
Gysbert Opdyck,
Jan Evertsen Bout,
Oloff Stevensen van Cortland.

The Nine Men.

Represented Manhattans, Breuckelen, Amersfoort and Pavonia, and the principal classes of the community, viz: the Merchants, Burghers and Agriculturists. The duties of this Board were: First, to promote the honor of God, the welfare of the country and the preservation of the Reformed Religion, according to the discipline of the Dutch Church. Second, to give their opinion on matters submitted to them by the Director and Council. Third, three of the nine, viz: one Merchant, one Burgher, one Farmer, were to attend for a month in rotation on the weekly Court, as long as civil cases were before it, and to act subsequently as Referees, or Arbitrators on cases referred to them. If in case of sickness or absence any of these three could not attend, his place was to be filled by another of the Nine Men of the same class. Six retired from office annually, to be replaced by an equal number selected from twelve names sent in by the whole Board. They held their sessions in David Provoost's School-room, and were the immediate precursors of the Burgomasters and Schepens, and of a Municipal form of government in the city of New Amsterdam.

1647 Sept. 25. Augustine Heerman,
    Arnoldus van Hardenbergh,
    Govert Loockermans, *Merchants.*
    Jan Jansen Damen, dead 1652.
    Jacob Wolfertsen (van Couwenhoven),
    Hendrick Kip, *Burghers.*

Michael Jansen,
Jan Evertsen Bout,
Thomas Hall, *Farmers*.

1649. Adriaen van der Donck, *President*,
Placed under arrest 4th March, 1649.

Augustine Heerman,
Arnoldus van Hardenbergh,
Govert Lockermans,
Oloff Stevensen van Cortland,
Hendrick Hendrickse Kip,
Michael Jansen,
Elbert Elbertsen (Stoothoff),
Jacob Wolfertsen van Couwenhoven.

1650 Augustine Heerman,
Jacob van Couwenhoven,
Elbert Elbertsen,
Hendrick Hendrickse Kip,
Michael Jansen,
Thomas Hall,
Oloff Stevens van Cortland,

NEW NETHERLAND REGISTER.

   Govert Loockermans,
   Jan Evertsen Bout.
1652 Feb. 2. David Provoost,
   William Beeckman,*
   Jacobus van Curler,
   Allard Anthony,
   Isaac de Foreest,
   Arent van Hattem,
   Jochem Pietersen Kuyter,
   Paulus Leendertsen van der Grist,
   Peter Cornelissen, the *Miller*.

---

* It appears that Mr. Beeckman came to New Netherland in 1647, in the ship Princess, in the West India Company service, but in what capacity is not stated. He was Lieutenant of the Burghers' Corps, New Amsterdam, in 1651; Schepen in 1653, 1654, 1656, and 1657; afterwards Commissary at the Delaware and at Esopus; Burgomaster in 1674, and after filling various other responsible offices, died in 1717.

BURGOMASTERS AND SCHEPENS.

New Amsterdam.

These functionaries succeeded the Nine men on the Incorporation of the city of New Amsterdam. They were appointed by the Director General and Council until January, 1656, when, on petition, they were allowed for the first time the privilege of nominating and submitting a double number to the Director and Council, from which the latter were to select the members of the Board for the ensuing year; but when the nomination was made, it was resolved on the 2d of February, by the Director and Council, "for concord and harmony's sake," some of those nominated having rendered themselves, by former disputes, unacceptable to the authorities, to continue the present Burgomasters and Schepens for another year, and only to supply the vacancies in the Board of Schepens by the nomination of two respectable persons. The nomination of their successors was not conceded until 1658. The incumbents entered office on 2d February of each year, unless otherwise stated.

BURGOMASTERS.

1653 Feb. 2. Arent van Hattem,
     Martin Cregier,

1654.		Arent van Hattem,
		Martin Cregier.
	Dec. 8.	Allard Anthony, *vice* Van Hattem returned to Holland.
•1655.		Allard Anthony,
		Oloff Stevensen van Cortland.
1656.		Allard Anthony,
		Oloff Stevensen van Cortland.
1657.		Allard Anthony,
		Paulus Lendertsen van der Grist.
1658.		Paulus Lendertsen van der Grist,
		Oloff Stevensen van Cortland.
1659.		Oloff Stevensen van Cortland,
		Martin Cregier.
1660.		Martin Cregier,
		Allard Anthony.
	April 26.	Oloff Stevensen van Cortland.*
1661.		Allard Anthony,
		Paulus Lendertsen van der Grist.

---

* Authorized to officiate as presiding Burgomaster, both these officers being absent. On 5th July, Burgomasters Cregier and Van Cortland accompanied the Director General to the Esopus for the purpose of concluding a peace with the Indians.

1662. Paulus Lendertsen van der Grist,
Oloff Stevensen van Cortland.
1663. Oloff Stevensen van Cortland,
Martin Cregier.
July 5. Paulus Lendertsen van der Grist,
vice Cregier.*
1664. Paulus Lendertsen van der Grist,
Cornelis Steenwyck.

1673 Aug. 17. Johannes van Brugh,
Johannes de Peyster,
Ægidius Luyck.
1674 Aug. 11. Johannes van Brugh,
William Beeckman.

SCHEPENS.

1653 Feb. 2. Paulus Lendertsen van der Grist,
Maximilian van Gheel,

---

* Entered the military service of the West India Company for the Esopus War.

Allard Anthony,*
William Beeckman,
Peter Wolfertsen van Couwenhoven.

1654. Paulus Lendertsen van der Grist†
William Beeckman,
Peter Wolfertsen van Couwenhoven,
Jochem Pietersen Kuyter,
Oloff Stevensen van Cortland.

Dec. 8. Joannes Nevius, *vice* Kuyter, murdered by Indians.

1655. Johannes Nevius,
Johannes de Peyster,
Johannes van Brugh,
Jacob Strycker,
Jan Vinge.

---

* 1653, last of June, was sent to Holland to obtain aid against the English, then threatening to invade New Netherland.

† Accompanied Director Stuyvesant to the West Indies 24th December, 1654.

1656.	Joannes van Brugh, </br> Jacob Strycker, </br> Jan Vinge, </br> William Beeckman, </br> Hendrick Hendricksen Kip.
1657.	William Beeckman, *President*. </br> Joannes de Peyster, </br> Govert Loockermans, </br> Adriaen Blommert, </br> Hendrick Jansen van der Vin.
1658.	Joannes de Peyster, *President*. </br> Peter Wolfertsen van Couwenhoven, </br> Jacob Strycker, </br> Cornelis Steenwyck, </br> Isaac de Foreest.
1659.	Peter Wolfertsen van Couwenhoven, </br> Joannes Pietersen van Brugh, </br> Jeronimus Ebbingh, </br> Hendrick Jansen van de Vin, </br> Jacob Kip.
1660.	Cornelis Steenwyck, *President*.

	Jacob Strycker,
	Govert Loockermans,
	Timotheus Gabry,
	Died 1680.
	Jacobus Backer.
1661.	Timotheus Gabry,
	Peter Wolfertsen van Couwenhoven,
	Johannes van Brugh,
	Jan Vinje,
	Jeronimus Ebbingh.
1662.	Johannes Pietersen van Brugh, *President*.
	Johannes de Peyster,
	Jacob Strycker,
	Jacob Backer,
	Isaac Grevenraet.
1663.	Jacob Strycker, *President*.
	Peter van Couwenhoven,
	Jan Vinje,
	Jacob Kip,
	Jacques Cousseau.

	July 5. Jacobus Backer, *vice* Couwenhoven.*
1664.	Jacobus Backer, *President*.
	Timotheus Gabry,
	Isaac Grevenraet,
	Nicolaus Meyer,
	Christoffel Hooglant.

1673 Aug. 17.	William Beeckman,
	Jeronimus Ebbingh,
	Jacob Kip,
	Lourens van der Spiegel,
	Gelyn Verplanck.
1674 Aug. 11.	Jacob Kip, *President*,
	Gelyn Verplanck,
	Francis Rombouts,
	Christoffel Hooglant,
	Stephen van Cortland.

* Entered the military service of the West India Company for the Esopus War.

ORPHAN MASTERS.

New Amsterdam.

The Deacons of the Church were considered the Guardians of Widows and Orphans. On the death of either a man or a woman, leaving children, they were bound to notify, through the Clerk of the church, the decease to the Director and Council, and afterwards in 1653 to the Burgomasters, who were *ex officio* Orphan Masters, and to apply for the appointment of Curators, unless the Orphan Court was specially excluded by the will of the deceased. The Burgomasters, who were burdened with many other duties, were subsequently relieved of the office of Orphan Masters at their own request, and persons specially appointed to discharge such duties. But the Burgomasters, notwithstanding, occasionally acted in the absence of the proper Orphan Masters. The number of the latter at first was two, but this was increased in 1658, to three, "as the business of the Court was largely augmented, in consequence of the great mortality that year." The legal powers and jurisdiction of the Court are very fully set forth in *Rooseboom's Recueil*, Chap. 28.

1653.   Burgomasters, *ex officio*, until
1655 Oct. 19. Peter Wolphertsen van Couwenhoven,
               Peter Cornelissen van der Veen.

1656 Feb. 25. Paulus Leendertsen van der Grist,
    Peter Wolphertsen van Couwenhoven.
1657 Feb. 13. Peter Wolphertsen van Couwenhoven,
    Oloff Stevensen van Cortland.
1658 Feb. 26. Peter Wolphertsen van Couwenhoven,
    Wilhelmus Beeckman.
Nov. 21. Peter Wolphertsen van Couwenhoven,
    Martin Cregier, *vice* Beeckman sent to the Delaware,
    Johannes Pietersen Verbrugge.
1659 Feb. Peter Wolphertsen van Couwenhoven,
    Johannes Pietersen Verbrugge,
    Allard Anthony.
Mar. 19. Paulus Leendertsen van der Grist.
May 7. Johannes de Peyster.
1660 Feb. 7. Paulus Leendertsen van der Grist,

Johannes de Peyster,
Oloff Stevensen van Cortland.

1661 Mar. 3. Oloff Stevensen van Cortland,
Martin Cregier,
Cornelis Steenwyck.

1662 Mar. 16. Martin Cregier,
Cornelis Steenwyck,
Peter Wolphertsen van Couwenhoven.

1663 Mar. 28. Allard Anthony,
Cornelis Steenwyck,
Johannes van Brugh.

Sept. 10. Govert Lookermans, *vice* Van Brugh gone to Fatherland.

1664 Mar. 18. Allard Anthony,
Govert Loockermans,
Jacob Strycker.

Fort Orange.

1652.   Vice Director, *ex officio*.
1657 Feb. 7. Jan Verbeeck,
Evert Wendel.

MAGISTRATES.

Fort Orange.

Two went out annually.

1654 April 14. Sander Leendertsen (Glen),
Pieter Hartgers,
Frans Barentsen Pastoor,
Jan Verbeeck,
Jan Tomassen,
Volckert Jansen.

1655 Aug. 11. Sander Leendertsen (Glen),
Peter Hartgers,
Frans Barentsen Pastoor,
Rutger Jacobsen, *vice* Verbeeck,
Andries Herbertsen, *vice* Tomassen,
Dirck Jansen Croon, *extra.*

1656 April 12. Rutger Jacobsen,
Andries Herbertsen,
Jacob Jansen Schermerhoorn, *vice* Leendertsen,
Philip Pietersen Schuyler, *vice* Hartgers,.

Goosen Gerritsen (van Schaack), *extra.*

1657 May 1. Jacob Jansen Schermerhoorn,
Philip Pietersen Schuyler,
Goosen Gerritsen, (van Schaack)
Abraham Staets, *vice* Jacobsen,
Jan Tomassen, *vice* Herbertsen,
Adriaen Gerritsen, *extra.*

1658 Mar. 26. Abraham Staets,
Jan Tomassen,
Adriaen Gerritsen,
Peter Hartgers, *vice* Schermerhoorn,
Francis Boon, *vice* Schuyler,
Dick Jansen Croon, *extra, vice* Gerritsen.

1659 May 1. Peter Hartgers,
Francis Boon,
Dirck Jansen Croon,
Andries Herbertsen, *vice* Staets,
Sander Leendertsen (Glen), *vice* Tomassen,
Jan Verbeeck, *vice* A. Gerritsen.

1660 April 12. Andries Herbertsen,
Sander Leendertsen (Glen),
Jan Verbeeck,
Rutger Jacobsen, *vice* Hartgers,
Frans Barentsen Pastoor, *vice* Boon,
Evert Jansen Wendel, *extra, vice* Croon.

1661 April 11. Rutger Jacobsen,
Frans Barentsen Pastoor,
Evert Jansen Wendel,
Abraham Staets,
Philip Pietersen Schuyler,
Adriaen Gerritsen, *extra.*

1662 April 6. Abraham Staets,
Adriaen Gerritsen,
Philip Pietersen Schuyler,
Francis Boon,
Goosen Gerritsen,
Jan Tomassen.

1663 April 5. Francis Boon,
Goosen Gerritsen,
Jan Tomassen,
Jan Verbeeck,

NEW NETHERLAND REGISTER.

              Gerrit Slechtenhorst,
              Stoffel Jansen.
1664 April 1. Jan Verbeeck,
              Gerrit Slechtenhorst,
              Stoffel Jansen,
              Jacob Schermerhoorn,
              Jan Hendricks van Bael,
              Jan Kostersen van Aecken.

Willemstadt.

1673 Oct. 6. Gerrit van Slechtenhorst,
              David Schuyler,
              Cornelis van Dyck,
              Peter Bogardus.

Schanegtede.

1673 Sept. 19. Sander Leendertsen Glen,
              Herman Vedder,
              Barent Janse.

[*Wiltwyck.*

1661 May 2. Evert Pels,
              Cornelis Barentsen Slecht,
              Albert Heymans.

1662.   Evert Pels,
        Tjerck Claessen de Witt,
        Albert Gysbertsen.
1663 April 5. Tjerck Claessen De Witt,
        Thomas Chambers,
        Albert Gysbertsen,
        Gysbert van Imbroch.
1664 April 3. Jan Willemsen Hooghteling,
        Hendrick Jochemsen.

Swaenenburgh.

1673 Oct. 6. Cornelis Wyncoop,
        Roeloff Kierstede,
        Wessel Ten Broeck,
        Jan Burhans.
1674 Aug. 14. Joost Adriaensen, vice Wyncoop,
        Cornelis Hoogeboom, *vice* Kierstede.

Hurley.

1673 Oct. 6. Louis du Bois,
        Roeloff Hendricksen.
1674 Aug. 14. Adriaen Albertsen Roosa, *vice* Du Bois.

Marbletown.

1673. Oct. 6. Jan Joosten,
            Jan Broersen.
1674 Aug. 14. William Jansen Schudt, *vice*
            Joosten.

Breuckelen.

1646 June 11. Jan Evertsen Bout,
            Huyg Aertsen van Rossum,
              Elected 21st May.
1653.   Jan Evertsen Bout,
            Frederick Lubbertsen,
              Died 1679.
1654 April 9. Jan Evertsen Bout,
              Reëlected; declined serving; died 1672.
            Frederick Lubbertsen,
            Albert Cornelissen Wantenaer,
            William Bredenbent,
            Joris Dircksen,
            Peter Cornelissen.
1655 April 13. Frederick Lubbertsen,
            Albert Cornelissen Wantenaar,
            Joris Dircksen,
            Joris Rapalje, *vice* P. Cornelissen.

1656 Mar. 28. Albert Cornelissen Wantenaar,
Joris Dircksen,
Joris Rapalje,
William Bredenbent, *vice* Lubbertsen.
1657 Mar. 27. Albert Cornelissen Wantenaar,
Joris Dircksen,
William Bredenbent,
Joris Rapalje.*
1658 Mar. 26. Joris Dircksen,
William Bredenbent,
Teunis Nyssen,
Peter Montfoort.
1659.

1660 May 3. Joris Dircksen,
William Bredenbent,
Joris Rapalje.

---

* A new nomination had been sent in, but as the majority of those named could neither read nor write, the old magistrates were continued.

1661 Mar. 21. Teunis Nyssen,
    William Gerritsen van Couwenhoven,
    Teunis Jansen,
    Thomas Verdon.

1662 Mar. 23. Teunis Jansen,
    William Gerritsen van Couwenhoven,
    Jan Jorissen Rapalje,
    Thomas Verdon.

1663 Mar. 19. Thomas Verdonck,
    William Bredenbent,
    Albert Cornelissen Wantenaar,
    Teunis Gysberts Bogaert.

1664 Mar. 20. Thomas Verdonck,
    William Bredenbent,
    Albert Cornelissen Wantenaar,
    William van Couwenhoven,
    Frederick Lubbertsen.

1673 Aug. 18. Theunis Gysbertse Bogaert,
    Frederick Lubbertse,

Thomas Lammertse,
Rem Jansen.

Midwout.

Planted 1652.

1654 Mar. 6. Jan Strycker,
Adriaen Hegeman,
Jan Snedicker.

1655 April 13. Jan Snedicker,
Adriaen Hegeman,
Thomas Swartwout, *vice* Strycker.

Oct. 16. Jan Strycker,
Adriaen Hegeman,
Thomas Swartwout.

1656 Mar. 28. Jan Snedicker,
Jan Strycker,
Peter Lott.

1657 Mar. 27. Jan Strycker,
Adriaen Hegeman,
William Jacobse van Boerum,
Jan Snedicker.

1658 Mar. 19. Adriaen Hegeman,
Jan Snedicker,

1659   William Guiljamsen.

1660 May 3. Jan Snedicker,
         Jan Strycker,
         William Willemse.
1661 Mar. 31.* Jan Snedicker,
         Jan Strycker,
         William Willemse.
1662 Mar. 23. Jan Strycker,
         William Jacobse van Boerum,
         Hendrick Jorissen.
1663 Mar. 19. Jan Snedicker,
         Hendrick Jorissen,
         William Jacobse van Boerum.
1664 Mar. 20. Jan Strycker,
         Jan Snedicker,
         William Guilliamsen.

---

* Previous to this date, there was only one Court of Justice for Midwout and Amersfoort, which sat three-fourths of the year at the former place, and one quarter at the latter; each now was granted a separate Court.

1673. Aug. 18. Hendrick Jorissen,
   Jan Strycker,
   Auke Jans,
   Peter Lott.

Amersfoort.

Planted 1633.

1654 April. Elbert Elbertsen (Stoothof),
   Nicholas Stillwell,
   Cornelis de Potter.
1655 April 13. Nicolas Stillwell,
   Peter Claessen, *vice* Elbertsen.

1656 Mar. 28. Elbert Elbertsen,
   Martin Jansen van Breuckelen.

1657 Mar. 27. Martin Jansen,
   Elbert Elbertsen (Stoothof),

1658 Mar. 19. Martin Jansen,
   Peter Claessen.

1659

NEW NETHERLAND REGISTER.

1660 April 24. Tunis Guisbert.
     May 3. Elbert Elbertsen,
         Peter Cornelissen,
         Simon Jansen van Aertsdalen.*
1661 Mar. 31. Elbert Elbertsen,
         Peter Cornelissen,
         Simon Jansen van Aertsdalen.
1662 Mar. 23. Elbert Elbertsen,
         Peter Cornelissen,
         Simon Jansen van Aertsdalen,
         Peter Claessen,
         Roelof Martensen van Breuckelen.
1663 Mar. 19. Elbert Elbertsen,
         Peter Claessen,
         Roelof Martense.
1664 Mar. 20. Elbert Elbertsen,
         Peter Cornelissen,
         Coert Stevensen.

---

* Amersfoort and Midwout had at this time but one joint Court of Justice, which sat at the latter place three quarters of a year, and only one quarter at Amersfoort. On application of the latter place, each village was provided with a subaltern Court, on 31st March, 1661.

1673 Aug. 18. Elbert Elbertsen,
Abram Jorissen,
Roelof Martensen,
Koert Stevensen.

New Utrecht.

Court erected February 23, 1660; incorporated 22d December, 1661.

1659. Jan Tomassen (van Dyck),
Jacobus van Corlear, *Superintendants.*
1660 Feb. 23. Jan Tomassen van Dyck.
Jacobus van Corlear.
1661 Dec. 22. Jan Tomassen (van Dyck),
Rutger Joosten van Brunt,
Jacob Hellakens, *alias* Swart.
1663 Jan. 4. Balthazar Vos,
Jacob Pietersen,
Francis de Bruyn.
1664 Jan. 10. Francis de Bruyn,
Balthazar Vos,
Jacob Hellakens.

1673 Aug. 18. Thomas Jansen,
           Hendrick Mattyssen (Smack),
           Jan Tomassen (van Dyck),
           Jan van Deventer.
Nov. 16. Jan Gysbertse van Meteren, *vice*
           Tomassen deceased.

Boswyck.

Court erected March 31, 1661.

1661 Mar. 31. Peter Jansen de Witt,
           Jan Tilje (Letelier),
           Jan Cornelissen Zeeuw.
1662 Mar. 30. Peter Jansen de Witt,
           Jan Cornelissen Zeeuw,
           Ryck Leydecker,
           Jan Catjouw.
Dec. 28. Jan Tiljer (Letelier), *vice* Catjou,
           returned to Holland.
1663 April 5. Gysbert Teunissen,
           Barent Joosten,
           Ryck Leydecker.
1664 April 3. David Jochimsen,
           John Lequier, of Paris.

1673 Aug. 18. Hendrick Barentse Smit,
Gysbert Theunissen,
Volckert Dirckse,
Jan Cornelissen de Zeeuw.

Gravesend.

Incorporated 1645.

1650. George Baxter,
William Wilkins,
Nicholas Stillwell.

Dec. A new Election was held, when other persons were chosen, but in consequence of Baxter's representations, they were not approved and the old magistrates held over.

1651. George Baxter,
William Wilkins,
Nicholas Stillwell.

James Hubbard,
William Bowne, *Assistants.*

1652.

1653.   George Baxter,*
        James Hubbard,*
        William Wilkins.

1654 Nov. 23. William Wilkins,
        The Sheriff and
        Town Clerk.

1655 July 19. William Bowne,
        William Wilkins,
        Edward Brouse.

1656 Mar. 25. William Bowne,
        William Wilkins,
        Edward Brouse.

1657 Mar. 27. Thomas Spicer,
        Nicolas Stillwell,
        William Bowne.

1658 July 4. Thomas Spicer,
        William Wilkins,
        Edward Brouse.

1659 April 21. William Wilkins,
        William Bowne,
        John Cooke.

1660.   William Wilkins.

---

* Removed from office for disaffection in 1654.

1661 Mar. 31. William Wilkins,
              John Cooke,
              William Bowne.
1662 May 4. William Wilkins,
              William Bowne,
              John Cooke.
1663 Jan.   William Wilkins,
              James Hubbard.*
     Nov.   Agents from Connecticut deposed the Magistrates in all the English villages under the Dutch, and appointed others in their stead.
1664 May 12. James Hubbard,†
              William Wilkins.†

1673 Aug. 18. Samuel Spicer,
              Richard Stillwell,

---

* Appointed by Captain John Scott.
† Appointed by Connecticut.

    John Emans,
    Barent Juriaensen.
1674 Sept. 6. Richard Stillwell,
    John Emans,
    John Tilton,
    Samuel Homs.

Middleburgh.

Planted 1642; incorporated 1652.

1652 Nov. 11. Thomas Hazard,
    Robert Coe,
    Richard Gildersleeve.
1653.   Thomas Hazard,
    Robert Coe,
    Bichard Gildersleeve.
1654.   Thomas Hazard,
    Robert Coe,
    Richard Gildersleeve.
1655.   Thomas Hazard,
    Robert Coe,
    Richard Gildersleeve.
1656 April 4. Robert Coe,
    Henry Feake,

	Richard Betts.
1657 June 12.	Henry Feake,
	Richard Betts,
	William Palmer.
1658 July 30.	William Palmer,
	John Coe,
	Edward Jessup.
1659.	Edward Jessup.
1660 July 5.	Magistrates of 1659, *continued*.
1661.	Edward Jessup,
	Ralph Hunt,
	John Coe,
	Jonathan Fish.
1662.	Edward Jessup,
	Ralph Hunt,
	John Coe,
	Jonathan Fish.
1663.	John Coe,
	Edward Jessup,
	Ralph Hunt,
	Richard Betts,

     Samuel Toe,
     John Layton,
     Francis Swaine.*
1663 Jan. 9. John Layton,
     Francis Swaine,
     William Blomfield,
     John Cochrane,
     Samuel Toe,
     Richard Betts,
     Ralph Hunt.†
1664 Feb. 20. John Burroughs,
     Ralph Hunt,
     John Ramsden,
     Samuel Toe,
     John Layton, *Townsmen.*
     Richard Betts,
     John Coe, *Magistrates.*‡

---

* These seven were townsmen to call meetings, &c.

† Elected overseers by the inhabitants in November, 1663. Agents from Connecticut removed the old Magistrates in all the English villages on Long Island under the Dutch, and appointed others in their stead.

‡ Elected under the presidency of Captain John Scott.

1664 May 12. Richard Betts,*
              John Coe.*

1673 Sept. 6. Richard Betts,
              Jonathan Hazard,
              Ralph Hunt.

Flushing.

Planted in 1645.

1648 April 27. John Tounsend,
              John Hicks,
              William Toorn.
1651,   John Underhill,
              Thomas Saul,
              Robert Terri,
1652,   John Hicks,

1655 April 22. Thomas Saul,
              William Laurence,
              Edward Farrington.

* Appointed by Connecticut.

1656 Mar. 25. William Laurence,
Edward Farrington,
William Noble.
1657. William Laurence,
Edward Farrington,
William Noble.
1658 Jan. 22. Court suspended in consequence of Messrs. Farrington and Noble remonstrating against the law against Quakers; the Court was restored
Mar. 26. William Lawrence,
Edward Farrington,
William Noble.*
1661. William Laurence,
Edward Farrington,
William Noble.
1662. William Laurence,
William Noble,

---

* No town meetings to be held without permission of the Director General and Council; in lieu thereof, seven Select men to be chosen to regulate, with the Magistrates, all matters relating to Roads, Fences, Bridges, Schools, Churches and other Public Buildings.

William Hallett.
1664 May 12. William Hallett,*
William Noble.*

1673 Aug. 30. John Hingsman [Hinchman],
Francis Bloetgoet,
Richard Wildie.

Hempstead.

Incorporated 16th November, 1644.

1647.   Richard Gildersleeve,
John Seaman,
John Hicks.

1652 April.   The Governor declared that the towne had not made a legall choyce [of Magistrates] and that all that they had done since Captaine Topping† went away, hee looked at it to bee as nothing, & wished them to make a new choyce.

---

* Appointed by Connecticut.
† Thomas Topping was Justice of Southampton from 1647 to 1663.

1652. Richard Gildersleeve,
Mr. Coe,
Daniel Whitehead.
1653 Dec. 11. John Stickland,
William Washburn,
Richard Gildersleeve.*
1654 Nov. 10. John Sumon [? Seaman,]
Robert Asiman† [Ashman.]
1655 Nov. 10. John Stickland,
John Hicks,
Richard Gildersleeve.
1656 Dec. 21. John Seaman,
Richard Gildersleeve,
John Hicks.
1657. Richard Gildersleeve,
John Seaman,
John Hicks.

---

* They were sworn to administer justice according to the tenor of their charter and the written laws of New Netherland, and authorized in case of sickness or absence, and on important cases, to adjoin one, two or three of the former magistrates to act for or with them.

† The magistrates ordered to send in a nomination for a third magistrate.

1658 Feb. 27. Richard Gildersleeve,
Robert Forman,
John Hicks.
Dec. 9. Richard Gildersleeve,
Robert Forman.
1659. John Hicks,
Robert Jackson.
1660 Dec. 15. John Hicks,
Robert Jackson,
Robert Ashman.
1661 May 2. Richard Gildersleeve,
John Hicks,
Robert Ashman.
1662 Feb. 6. John Hicks,
Robert Ashman,
Robert Jackson.
1663 Jan. 20. John Hicks,
Richard Gildersleeve,
Robert Ashman.
1664 May 12. John Hicks,*
Richard Gildersleeve, senr.*

---

* Appointed by Connecticut.

1673 Aug. 30. John Smith, senr.,
          John Semmens [Seaman,]
          William Jacobs.
    Sept. 25. Robert Jackson, *vice* Smith.

Rustdorp.

           Granted March 21, 1656.
1659.   Benjamin Coe,
           Samuel Mathews,
           Richard Everett.
1659 Sept. 9. Samuel Mathews,
           John Townsend,
           Benjamin Coe.
1661 Jan. 24. Richard Everett,
           Nathaniel Denton,
           Andrew Messenger,
      In the room of others who had connived with Quakers.
1662 Jan. 28. In consequence of continued dissensions among the People and Magistrates, on account of the Quaker prosecutions, a special officer was sent down to take possession of all the Records of

1662 Jan. 28. the Town, then in the hands of Nathaniel Denton, and to order a nomination to be made by all the Freemen of the true and Protestant religion, of four persons, out of whom and the present Magistrates others were to be appointed for the ensuing year. March 16, 1662, Records ordered to be delivered to Mr. Coe, actual Magistrate and the oldest Inhabitant of the place.

1662 Mar. 4. Robert Coe,
Daniel Denton,
Andrew Messenger.

1663 Mar. 20. Robert Coe,
John Stickland,
Thomas Benedict.

1664 May 12. Robert Coe,*
Thomas Benedict.*

---

* Appointed by Connecticut.

1673 Aug. 30. John Carpenter,
Robert Ashman,
Nathaniel Denton.

Oysterbay.

Had never been under the Dutch Government until 1673.

1661 May 9. No Court established here.
1662 July 22. John Rigebell.
1664 May 12. Jno Rickbell*
Robert Ferman.*
1673 Aug. 30. Nicolas Wright,
Thomas Tounsen,
Nathaniel Coles.

Huntington.

1673 Sept. 8. Joseph Whiteman,
Isaac Platt.
1674. Jonas Wood,
James Chichester.

Seatalcot.

1673 Sept. 8. Richard Woodhil,
John Bayles.

---

* Appointed by Connecticut.

Southampton.

1673 Sept. 8. Edward Howell,
Josuah Barens.

Easthampton.

1673 Sept. 8. John Mulford,
John Stretton.

Southold.

1673 Sept. 8. Thomas More,
Refused to serve.
Thomas Hudsisson.

Haerlem.

Court erected 16th August, 1660.

1660 Aug. 16. Jan Pietersen Slot,
Daniel Terneur,
Peter Cresson.
1661 Nov. 3. Jan Pietersen Slot,
Daniel Terneur,
Johannes La Montagne, junr.,
vice Cresson.
1662 Nov. 16. Johannes La Montagne, junr.
Philip Cassie.

              Dirck Claessen.
1663 April 23. Michel Muyden.
    Nov. 17. Jan La Montagne,
             Daniel Terneur,
              Johannes Verveelen,
              John Pietersen Slot.

1673.   Resolved Waldron,
              David des Marest,
              Joost van Oblinis,
              Arent Hermans.
1674 Oct. 2. Jan Petersen Harling,
              Adriaen Cornelissen,
              Jacob Pietersen de Groot,
              Wolfert Webber.

Westchester.

1656 Mar. 16. Thomas Wheeler.
    Mar. 28. Thomas Wheeler,
             Thomas Newman,
                Died 1660, aged 76 years.
              John Lord.

1657.   Thomas Newman,
                John Lord,
                John Smith.
1660 Jan. 21.   Josias Gilbert,
                Nicolas Bayley,
                Thomas Veall.
1661 Jan. 11.   Thomas Mollinaer,
                Thomas Vaile,
                Edward Waters.
1662 Feb. 15.   Edward Waters,
                Robert Huestis,
                William Betts.
1663 May 24.   Robert Huestis,
                John Barker,
                Nicholas Bayley.
     Oct. 8.   Edward Gishop (Jessup).*
1664 May 12.   Edward Jessup.*

1673 Aug. 30.   Joseph Palmer,
                Edward Waters,
                Richard Pampton.

* Appointed by Connecticut,

Mamaroneck.

1673 Aug. 24. John Busset,
Henry Disbrow.

Fordham.

1673 Oct. 18. Johannis Verveelen,
Michael Bastiaensen,
Valentine Claessen.

Eastchester.

1673 Aug. 30. John Hoit.

Staten Island.

1664 Jan. 28. David D'amarex,
Pierre Billiou,
Walraven Lutten.

1673 Aug. 25. Tys Barentse van Leerdam,
Jan Willemse.
1674 Feb. 14. Gideon Marlet,
Nathan Whiteman, *additional.*

Bergen.

1661 Feb. 10. Tielman van Vleeck, *President*.
  Herman Smeeman,
  Caspar Steinmits,
  Michel Jansen.
1662 Oct. 16. Caspar Steinmits,
  Engelbert Steenhuysen,
  Gerrit Gerritsen.
1663 Dec. 17. Balthazar Bayard,
  Adolph Hardenbrook,
  Harman Smeeman.

1673 Aug. 18. Gerrit Gerritse,
  Thomas Fredericks,
  Elias Michielse,
  Peter Marcellissen,
  Cornelis Abramse.
1674 Aug. 31. Walinck Jacobse,
  Engelbert Steenhuys.

Gemoenepas.

1674 Aug. 31. Enoch Michielse.

Ahasymus.

1674 Aug. 31. Claes Jansen.

Minckaque and Pemrepoch.

1674 Aug. 31. Jan Dircksen Siecken.

Elizabethtown.

1673 Aug. 24. John Ogden, senr.,
Samuel Hopkins,
Jacob Melyn.

New-Worke.

1673 Aug. 24. Jasper Crane,
Robert Bond,
John Ward.

Shrewsbury.

1673 Aug. 24. John Hanoe,
Eleakim Wardil,
Hugh Dyckman.*

---

* These persons not being allowed by their religion to take, or to administer an oath, were discharged and a new election ordered 29th September, 1673.

Piscataway.

1673 Aug. 25. John Smally,
Nicholas Boman,
Daniel Denton.

Tinnacung, (on the Delaware).

1658. Oloff Stive (Stille),
Matys Hansen,
Peter Rambo,
Resigned 21st March, 1661.
Peter Kaick (Cock).
1662. Joost La Grange.

New Amstel.

1661. Johannes Hendricks,
Peter Petersen Harder.
1660 June 29. Hendrick Kip,
Jacob Crabbe,
Bores Joosten.

Whorekil.

1673. Harmanus Wiltbanck,
Sander Maelstyn,

John Roots (Rhodes),
William Claessen.

TOWN CLERKS.

New Amsterdam.

1653 Jan. 27. Jacob Kip.
1657 June 13. Timotheus Gabry.
1658. Johannes Nevius.

New Orange.

1673. Nicholas Bayard.
1674. Ephraim Hermans, *Deputy.*

Haerlem.

1673. Hendrick van der Vin.

Fort Orange.

1654. Peter Ryverdingh.
1656 Sept. 28. Johannis Provoost.
1673 Oct. 6. Johannes Provoost.

Renselaerswyck.

1630.	Arent van Corlear.
1642.	Anthony de Hooges.*
1656.	———— van Hamel.
1660.	Dirck van Schelluyne.

Esopus.

1658.	Mathys Capito.
1663 June 14.	Mathys Capito.
1673 Oct. 7.	William La Montagne.

Breuckelen.

1654.	The Sheriff, *ex officio*.
166–.	Michel Hainelle.

Boswyck.

1661.	Senior Magistrate.
1663 April 5.	B. Hanout.

Amersfoort.

1663 Mar. 19.	Adrian Hegeman.

---

* Landed at the Manhattans 29th November, 1641; his widow married Roelof Swartwout.

New Utrecht.

1662.　　　　Jacob van Corlear.

Gravesend.

1650.　　　　John Tilton.
1662.　　　　William Goulding.
1673 Aug. 18. Francis de Bruyn.*

Flushing.

1648 April 27. John Lawrence.
1657.　　　　Edward Heart.
1662.　　　　Edward Fisher.

Middleburgh.

1655.　　　　William Wood.
1659.　　　　Thomas Lawrence.
1662 Mar. 13. John Burroughs.
1663 Sept.　　James Bradish.

Hempstead.

1647.　　　　John James.
1650.　　　　Daniel Denton.

---

* He was Clerk also of the Five Dutch Towns.

1657.   John James.
1660 Dec. 15.   Robert Maruine.
1661.   Jonas Holdsworth.

Rustdorp.

I doubt if there was any Town Clerk proper in this Town; one of the Magistrates seems to have acted in that capacity.

1657 Feb. 18.   Daniel Denton.
1661.   Nathaniel Denton.
1662.   Robert Coe.

Oysterbay.

1673.   Mathias Harvey.

The Five English Towns.*

1673 Aug. 31.   Carel van Brugge.

Southampton.

1673.   John Laughton.

Seatalcot.

1673.   Nathaniel Brewster.

---

* Flushing, Hempstead, Rustdorp, Middleburgh and Oysterbay.

Easthampton.

1673.   Thomas Talmadge.

Huntington.

1673.   Thomas Powell.

*Towns on East End of Long Island.**

1673 Sept. 8. Henry Pierson.

Westchester.

1661.   Richard Mills.

Fordham.

1673 Oct. 18. Johannes Verveelen.

Staten Island.

1673 Aug. 25. Peter Biljou.

Bergen.

1664 Mar. 17. Balthazar Bayard.
1673 Aug. 18. Claes Arentse Stoers.

---

* Southampton, Seatalcot, Huntington, Easthampton and Southold.

Achter-Col.

1673 Sept. 1. Samuel Hopkins.

New-Work.

1673.　　　　John Browne, jr., *Recorder.*

Fort Casimir and New Amstel.

1655.　　　　Andries Hudde.
1655 Sept. 1. Jan Juriaens Becker.
1659.　　　　Cornelis van Gezel.
　　　　　　　Abraham van Nes.
1660 Jan.　　Gerrit van Sweringen.
1661.　　　　C. J. Verbraack,
　　　　　　　R. Ravens.

Altona.

1658.　　　　Jan Juriaensen Becker, *Commissary.*
1660 June 5. Andries Hudde, *vice* Becker dismissed.

TOWN TREASURERS.

New Amsterdam.

1655. The retiring Burgomaster.

Fort Orange.

1659 Dec. 2. Francis Boon.

COURT MESSENGERS.

The duties of these Officers were to serve Summons, make Arrests, levy Executions, &c., and were similar to those of a Marshal or Constable of the present day. In the English towns on Long Island they were, in fact, called and known as Constables.

To the Council.

1638. Philip de Truy.
1654. Claes van Elsland.
1656. Simon Joosten,
       Claes van Elsland, junr.
1658 April 16. Peter Schaefbanck,
       Gysbert Opdyck.

New Amsterdam.

1655 Feb. 6. Dirck van Schelluyne.
1656 Nov. 6. Mattheus de Vos.

Fort Orange.

1654. Peter Ryverdingh.
1656 Aug. 7. Ludovicus Cobes.

Rensselaerswyck.

1662. Anthony Jansen.

Breuckelen.

1657. Simon Joosten.
1664 July 4. Carel de Beauvois.

Middleburgh.

1654. Elias Bayley.

Flushing.

1658. John Mastine.

Hempstead.

Richard Valentine.

Oysterbay.

1662 July 22. John Rigebell.*

Bergen.

1663.   Claes Arentse Stoers.

New Amstel.

1656 Jan. 19. Mathys Bouchesne.
1661.   Hendrick Gerritsen van Gezel.
1662.   Gerrit de Groot.

PROVOST MARSHAL.

1647 Feb. 28. Peter Ebel.
  June 14. Adam Roelantsen.
1654 Aug. 23. Arent Jansen van Vlieringen.
1655 Nov. 29. Israel Bensen Volck, *vice* Jansen, absconded.
1656 Jan. 18. Dirck Crynen, *vice* Volck absconded.
1658 May 25. Resolved Waldron *vice* Crynen returned to Fatherland.

---

* Appointed by Connecticut.

1655.   Anthony Lodewycksen Baeck,
            Burgher Provost.

JAILER.

1646.   Jan Pietersen, from Amsterdam.
1657 Feb. 6.   Anthony Lodewicksen Baeck.

TURNKEY.

1653.   Dirck Crynsen.
1661 Feb. 24.   Peter Bastiaensen.

TOWN CRIER.

1655 Dec. 23.   Christoffel Michielsen, in place of his predecessor who returned to Holland.

FIRE WARDENS.

New Amsterdam.

1648 Jan. 23. Adriaen Keyser,
   Thomas Hall,
   Martin Cregier,
   George Wolsey.
1655 April 13. Hendrick Kip,
   Govert Loockermans,
   Jean Paul Jacquet.
1656 Jan. 18. Christian Barentsen, *vice* Jacquet.
1657 Feb. 13. Daniel Litscho, *vice* Lookermans.
1658 Dec. 23. Jan Jansen de Jongh,
   Johannis de La Montagne, junr.
1661 Jan. 20. Evert Duyckingh.
   Mar. 3. Hendrick Willemsen Backer,
   Claes Gangeloffsen.

1674 Jan. 5. Jan Jansen van Bresteede,
   Evert Duyckingh,
   Rynier Willemsen Backer,
   Jonas Bartelse.

VENDUE MASTERS.

This office and its perquisites belonged, *ex officio*, to the Provincial Secretary, who performed its duties by Deputy. After the organization of a municipal government for New Amsterdam, a question arose as to whether the City Clerk, or the Secretary of the Province was Vendue Master within the City limits. It was then adjudged by the Supreme Court, that the sale of property, both real and personal, under judgment of the Director and Council, belonged to the Secretary of the Province, or his Deputy Vendue Master. The City Clerk was Vendue Master to the Court of Orphans, and in cases where judgment had been rendered by the Court of Burgomasters and Schepens.

Secretary of the Province, *ex officio*
1649. Adriaen Keyser, *Deputy*.
1661. Timotheus Gabry, *Deputy*.
1672. Jacques Corteljou, L. I.
1673 Aug. 20. Nicholas Bayard, *Secretary*.
1674 Jan. 1. Francis de Bruyn, for the Five Dutch Towns on Long Island, *vice* Corteljou.

New Amsterdam.

1655 Nov. 29. City Clerk.

ROY MASTERS, OR CITY SURVEYORS.

1647 July 22. Lubbertus van Dincklagen,
    Paulus Leendertsen van der Grist
    Cornelis van Tienhoven.
1655 Mar. 2. Peter Wolfertsen van Couwenhoven, *vice* Dincklagen.
1655 Nov. 10. Johannes de La Montagne,
    Allard Anthony.
1656. Paulus Leendersten van der Grist
1657 Feb. 13. Hendrick Hendricksen Kip, *vice* Van der Grist.

INSPECTORS.

Here we have the introduction of those Inspection Laws which continued in this State for more than two hundred years, and were abolished only by the Constitution of 1846.

Of Tobacco.

1638 Aug. 12. Claes van Elsland,
    Wibrant Pietersen.
1640 Jan. 5. Jacob van Curler,

David Provoost, *vice* Elsland and Pietersen.
1653. Isaac de Foreest,
George Holmes.
1655 April 13. Peter van der Linde, *vice* Holmes.

Of Beer Barrels.

1656 Nov. 28. Jacob Jansen van Noorstrande.

Of Bread.

1661 Oct. 13. Hendrick Willemsen, *Baker*, Christoffel Hoogland.

Of Weights and Measures.

1657 Jan. 8. Warnaer Wessels.

Measurers of Grain and Lime.

1657 Feb. 6. Jacob Leendersten van der Grist, Michiel Jansen.
1658 Feb. 21. Joannes Leendertsen van der Grist.

MILLERS.

1638.	Abraham Pietersen.
1640.	Philip Gerritsen.
1652.	Peter Cornelissen.
1655.	Abraham Martins Clock.
1661.	Jan De Witt.

FERRY MASTERS.

Ferries were leased, or let to farm, for a certain number of years.

To Long Island.

1652.	Cornelis Dircksen Hooglant.
1654.	Egbert van Borsum.
1662.	Paulus van der Beeck.

To Bergen.

1661.	William Jansen.

CLERGYMEN.

Reformed Dutch.

New Amsterdam.

1628.	Jonas Michaëlius.
1633.	Everardus Bogardus, Drowned 1647.
1647.	Joannes Backerus.
1649.	Joannes Megapolensis, Died 1669.
1652.	Samuel Drisius.
1659 Aug.	Machiel Zyperus.*
1664.	Ægidius Luyck, *Rector of Latin School.*
	Samuel Megapolensis.†

Pavonia.

1633.	Michel Pauluszoon.

---

* Previously Minister at Curaçao, which Island he now left for New Netherland, "in the hope of receiving a call there." His hope does not appear to have been realized.

† Returned to Holland.

Rensselaerswyck and Fort Orange.

1642. Joannes Megapolensis.
1650. Wilhelmus Grasmeer.*
1652. Gideon Schaets.

Midwout and Dutch Towns on Long Island.

1654. Johannes Theodorus Polhemus,
Died 1676.

Breuckelen.

1660. Henricus Selyns,
Died 1701.

Esopus.

1660. Hermanus Blom.*

New Amstel (Delaware).

1657. Everardus Welius,
Died 9th December, 1659.

---

* Returned to Holland.

Independent.

Hempstead.

1644.	Richard Denton, Returned to England.
164–.	Robert Fordham, Went to Southampton in 1649.
1661.	Jonah Fordham.

Middleburgh.

1642.	Francis Doughty.
1652.	John Moore, Died 1657.
1657.	Richard Mills, Schoolmaster, officiated on Sundays, until
1662.	William Leverich.

Flushing.

1646–7.	Francis Doughty, Went to Maryland, 164$\frac{8}{9}$.
1656.	William Wickendam, *Baptist;* banished.

Jamaica.

1662.	Zachariah Walker.

Westchester.

1656. No Minister; meetings held on the Sabbath, when Mr. Bailey made prayer, and Robert Bassett read a sermon.

LUTHERAN.

New Amsterdam.

1657. Joannes Ernestus Goetwasser; banished.

Fort Christina (Delaware).

1637. Reorus Torkillus.
1643. John Campanius,
Left in 1648.
1650. Laurence Charles Lokenius, and two other Ministers.*

New Amstel.

1663 June 6. Abelius Zetskoorn.

---

* These two were sent back to Sweden in 1655.

Catholic.

These Clergymen, except Fathers Bressani and Poncet, who were prisoners, acted as Missionaries among the Iroquois, or Five Nations of Indians.

1642.	Isaac Jogues, S. J.
	Put to death 1646.
1644.	Joseph Bressani, S. J.
1653.	Joseph Poncet, S. J.
1654.	Simon Le Moyne, S. J.
1655.	Peter J. M. Chaumonot, S. J.
1655.	Claude Dablon, S. J.
1656.	Francois Le Mercier, S. J.
1656.	Réné Menard, S. J.
1656.	Jacques Fremin, S. J.
1657.	Paul Ragueneau, S. J.
	Francis Duperon, S. J.
1661.	Simon Le Moyne, S. J.

Advocates.

	Adriaen van der Donck.
1652.	Cornelis de Potter.
1653.	Francis Le Bleu.

NOTARIES.

New Amsterdam.

1651 Sept. 9. Dirck van Schelluyne,
                Arrived in New Netherland in 1652.
1652 Sept. 16. David Provoost.
1655 April 13. Johannes de Decker.
1656 April 4. Mattheus de Vos.
1656 Oct. 31. Pelgrom Clock.
1658 July 30. Tielman van Vleck, from Bremen.
1661 Jan. 19. Solomon La Chaire.
1662 Jan. 19. Walewyn van der Veen.
1673 Dec. 21. Allard Anthony.

Delaware.

1659.   Abraham van Nas.

Willemstadt.

1673 Nov. 2. Lodewyck Cobes.

Schenectady.

1673.   John Gerritsen van Marck.

PHYSICIANS AND SURGEONS.

The first members of the Medical profession in New Netherland were, of course, Ship Surgeons who practised on shore whilst their vessels lay in port. Some of these settled at the Manhattans and eked out a subsistence by being sometimes employed by the government. The following extract from the Dutch Records, illustrates the state of the Profession in those days:

"1652, February 2. On the petition of the Chirurgeons of New Amsterdam, that none but they alone be allowed to shave; the Director and Council understand that Shaving doth not appertain exclusively to Chirurgery, but is an appendix thereunto; that no man can be prevented operating on himself, nor to do another this friendly act, provided it be through courtesy and not for gain, which is hereby forbidden." It was then further

Ordered, That Ship-Barbers shall not be allowed to dress any wounds, nor administer any potions on shore, without the previous knowledge and special consent of the Petitioners, or at least of Doctor La Montagne.

This is the earliest order on record regulating the Practice of Medicine in the State. In 1658, Messrs. Kierstede, Varrevanger and L'Oragne were the only Surgeons in New Amsterdam.

New Amsterdam.

1630.   Herman Mynderts van den Bogaert.

1637. Johannes La Montagne,
　　　　Member of the Supreme Council and Vice Director of Fort Orange.

1638. Hans Kierstede,
　　　　Died in 1671.

　　　　Peter van der Linde,
　　　　Gerrit Schut,
　　　　Jan Pietersen van Essendelft,
　　　　Died in 1640.

1644. Paulus van der Beeck, from Bremen.
　　　　Had served in Curaçao and on board the Company's ships; settled finally in Breuckelen.

1647. William Hays, of Barry's Court, Ireland.
　　　　Served since 1641, as Chief Surgeon in Curaçao.

　　　　Peter Vreucht.

1649. Jacob Hendricksen Varrevanger,
　　　　Entered the Company's service in 1646, discharged June 1662.

　　　　Isaac Jansen (*ship*),
　　　　Jacob Mollenaer (*ship*),
　　　　Jan Pauw (*ship*).

1652.   Jan Herwy (Hervey),
                William Noble (*ship*),
                Gysbert van Imbroch.
1655.   Jacobus Hugues,
                Johannes Megapholensis, junr.,
                    Returned to Holland, *circa* 1656.
                M. Cornelis Clock.
1658 Nov. 18.   Peter Jansen van den Bergh,
                Jacob L'Oragne.
1659.   Alexander Carolus Curtius.
1660.   Harman Wessels.
1662.   Jan du Parck (*military*),
                Samuel Megapolensis,
                Cornelis van Dyck,
                    Died 1687.
1673.   Henry Taylor.

Fort Orange.

1642.   Abraham Staets.
1655.   Jacob d'Hinse.

Esopus.

1660.   Gysbert van Imbroch.
1664 July 17.   Sybrant Cornelissen van Flensburgh.

Middleburgh.

1662. James Clark,
—— Folcks, *Mespath.*
1663. William Leverich.*

Delaware.

1655. Jan Oosting,
—— Rynvelt,
Died August, 1658.
William van Rasenburgh.
1657. David Ludekens,
1660. Tymen Stodder.
1662. Jacob de Kommer.

MATRON OF THE ORPHANS.
SENT FROM AMSTERDAM.
1654. Immetje Cornelis.

---

* A supply of drugs was sent from Holland in the spring of this year, for an English Clergyman, "versed in the art of Physick and willing to serve in the capacity of Physician." The Rev. William Leverich is supposed to be the Clergyman alluded to. He had sailed in October, 1660, from New Amsterdam for Holland, in the ship Spotted Cow, and returned in the fall or winter of 1662.

MIDWIVES.

Midwives in Holland, before being licensed, were duly examined by a board of Physicians. One of such licensed women was appointed Midwife to a Town or Village. This custom was transferred to New Netherland.

New Amsterdam.

163–. Tryn Jansen (or Jonas).
    She was the mother of the much talked of Annetje Jans, wife of Rev. Everardus Bogardus, and died in 1647.

1638. Lysbet Dircksen.
1655 April 21. Hellegonda Joris.

Esopus.

1655. Mrs. Cornelis Barentsen Slecht.

MATRON OF THE HOSPITAL.*

1658 Dec. 23. Hilletje Wilburch.

---

* This Hospital was established at the request of Surgeon Hendricksen Varrevanger for the reception of sick Soldiers, who had been previously billeted on private families, and of the Company's Negroes, who were left destitute in case of sickness. It was the first Hospital on the Island of Manhattan.

SCHOOLMASTERS.

"School-keeping and the appointment of Schoolmasters depend absolutely," say the Dutch Records, "from the *Jus Patronatus*, and require a License from the Director General and Council." In New Netherland, as in Holland, Church and State were intimately allied, and the office of Teaching thus became, in some respects, semi-ecclesiastical. The duties of the Parochial Schoolmaster, as set forth in his commission, were to promote Religious Worship, to read a portion of the Word of God to the people, to endeavor as much as possible to bring them up in the ways of the Lord, to console them in their Sickness and to conduct himself with all diligence and fidelity in his calling, so as to give others a good example, as becometh a devout, pious and worthy Consoler of the Sick, Church Clerk, Precentor and Schoolmaster, in which capacities all persons, without distinction, were commanded to acknowledge him. These, however, were the duties only of Teachers of Schools belonging to, or under Consistories or Churches, or who were appointed to Towns or settlements not yet provided with a Minister. Teachers of Private Schools, though necessarily licensed, were not connected officially with the Church.

New Amsterdam.

1633. Adam Roelantsen,
Resigned in 1639.

1643.		John Stevensen,
		Resigned in 1648.
1647 Nov.		For want of a proper place, no School has been kept in three months.
		Aryaen Jansen.
		David Provoost.
1648 Oct. 26.		Peter van der Linde, *vice* Stevensen.
1649.		Jan Cornelissen,*
		Adriaen van Ilpendam,
		Joost Carelse.
1650.		Schoolmaster sent from Holland.
1652 April.		Johannes Momie de La Montagne.
	Sept.	Hans Steyn.
1654 Dec. 3.		Andries Hudde petitions for leave to keep a School; is referred to the Ministers of the Church.
1655 Jan. 26.		William Verstius
		Requests his discharge.

---

* The other Teachers, says Secretary Van Tienhoven, keep school in hired houses, so that the youth are not in want of Schools to the extent of the circumstances of the country.

1655 Mar. 23. Harmen van Hoboken, *vice* Verstius.
1658 Jan. Jacobus van Corlear;
Feb. 19. Is ordered to discontinue teaching, until he obtain proper authority so to do. Feb. 26, petitions for leave, and *nihil actum* thereupon. Mar. 26, permission peremptorily refused.
Aug. 13. Jan Lubberts.
1659 April 16. Alexander Carolus Curtius, *Rector of Latin School.**
1660 Aug. 15. Jan Juriaense Becker.
Frans Claessen,
Died before 1662.
1661 May 2. Evert Pietersen.
Oct. 27. Harmen van Hoboken, *Bowery.*
1662 April Ægidius Luyck, *Rector of Greek and Latin School.*
Sept. 21. Johannes van Gelder.†

---

* Had previously been a professor in Lithuania; arrived at the Manhattans in July, 1659; resigned and returned to Holland in 1660.

† 1662, Feb. 2. Part of the old Burying ground is granted to the Burgomasters of New Amsterdam for the purpose of erecting a Public School house.

Haerlem.

1664 Jan. 10. Johannis La Montagne.

Fort Orange.

1650 Sept. 9. Andries Jansen.

Esopus.

1658. Andries van der Sluys.

Midwout.

1655 Oct. 16. Lot reserved for Schoolmaster.
1659. Adriaen Hageman; to 1671.
1660. Renier ———

Middleburgh.

1660. Richard Mills.

Breuckelen.

1661 July 4. Carel de Beauvois.*

Boswyck.

1662 Dec. 28. Boudewyn Maenhout.

---

* Court messenger, precentor, bellringer, gravedigger, and schoolmaster.

Bergen.

1662 Oct. 6. Englebert Steenhuysen.

New Amstel, (Delaware).

1657 April   Evert Pietersen.
1661.   Arent Evertsen Molenaar.

INDIAN INTERPRETERS.

To Algonquins, unless otherwise stated.

1645. Jan Evertsen Bout,
Claes Jansen Ruyter.
1645. Cornelis Anthonissen, *for Mohawks*.
1646. Simon Root,
Jan Hendricksen,
Dirck Dirksen Coe, *for Mohawks*.
1656. Laurens Hansen.
1658. Govert Loockermans,
Peter Wolphertsen van Couwenhoven,
Claes Cartense,
Wharinus van Courbe.

1660 Mar. 1.	Claes Jansen Ruyter,
	Jan David.
1663.	Sara Kierstede,*
	Peter Ebel,
	Harmen Douwesen,
	Tryntie Geerts.
1673.	Sara van Borsum.*
1674.	Jan Janse Bleeker,
	Hendrick Lantsingh.

OVERSEERS

Of Laborers.

1633.	Claes Jacobsen from Schagen,
	Jacob Stoffelsen.
1639 Aug. 11.	Gillis de Voocht.
1647 Jan. 10.	Paulus Heyman, *of Negroes;*
	Resigned 1656.
1656.	Resolved Waldron.
1660.	Paulus Heyman.

* The same person.

Of Masons.

1638 May 10. Hendrick Pietersen.
1647 July 25. William Pietersen from Bossaert.
1661. Peter Jansen.

Of Carpenters.

1638 June 1. Gillis Pietersen,
    Aug. 1. Thomas Walraven.
1642. Jan Dircksen,
    Tymen Jansen, *Ship Carpenter.*
1645 May 11. Peter Cornelissen.
1653. Jan Engelbrecht.
1655. Jan Jansen Westerhout.
1659. Mangnus Mangnussen.
1673 Sept. 26. Adrian Jansen from Westerhout,
    Hendrick van Borsum.

Of Coopers.

1658. Fredrick Hendricksen.

Of Bakers.

1656. Frederick Barents.
1658 Feb. 26. Hendrick Willemsen.

Of Smiths.

1648.   Barent Ennesen from Noorden.
1656 June 19. Dirck Houthuysen.

PROVINCIAL AGENTS.

To Holland.

On the part of the Commonalty.

1649 July 26. Adriaen van der Donck,
            Jacob van Couwenhoven,
            Jan Evertsen Bout.

On the part of the Government.

    Sept.   Cornelis van Tienhoven.
1653 June 30. Allard Anthony.

On the part of the Convention.

1653 Dec.   Francis de Bleuw.

1655 Oct. 31. Cornelis Jacobsen Steenwyck.
1663 Nov. 1. Jeremias van Rensselaer,
            Johan Pietersen van Brugh,
            Jacob Backer.

1664 April 26. Cornelis van Ruyven,*
              Cornelis Steenwyck.*

AMBASSADORS.

To Rhode Island.

1651 Oct. 31 Cornelis van Tienhoven.
1652 April.   Adriaen Keyser,
              Augustine Heermans.

To New Haven.

To explain Measures adopted against Pirates.

1654 April 14. Cornelis van Tienhoven,
              Martin Cregier.
1655.   Delegates were sent this year to New England to engage those Colonies in a league offensive and defensive against the Indians, but we have not their names.

---

* Appointed but did not go.

To Maryland.

1659 Sept.   Augustine Heermans, *
              Resolved Waldron.

To Virginia.

To negotiate a Treaty of Peace and Commerce.

1653 May.   Cornelis van Tienhoven,
             Arent van Hattem.

To obtain an Answer to the above Proposals; meanwhile to request free intercourse and trade.

1653 Dec. 16. Samuel Drisius.

To condole the Death of Governor Matthews, to conclude a Commercial Treaty and enlist soldiers.

1660 Feb. 27. Nicolas Varlet,
              Brian Newton.

To reclaim the ship "Arms of Amsterdam," seized by a Portuguese privateer and carried thither.

1663 Nov.   Johannes de Decker,
             Nicolas Varlet,
             Jacobus Backer.

From Connecticut.

To learn on what terms the Dutch would vacate the land around Fort Good Hope.

1642 July 10. Mr. Hill,
Mr. Whiting.

From Virginia.

1647. George Grace.
1660 May 18. Sir Henry Moody, Bart.

From Canada.

1657. Simon Le Moyne, S. J.

From Massachusetts.

1659 Nov. 12. William Hawthorne.
John Richards.

CONVENTIONS.

1653 Sept. Delegates from the respective Colonies and Courts of New Netherland, met in the course of this month at New Amsterdam and, with the Director General and Council, enacted divers Ordinances and Regulations providing against the great and excessive dearness of all sorts of merchandise, provisions, grain and wages. This may be considered, then, as the *First Legislative* Assembly within the confines of the present State of New York. The names of the Delegates are not on record.

1653 October. Delegates from Hempstead, Gravesend, Flushing, and Middleburgh, whose names are not known, met about this month, at the last named place, to

1653 Oct. consider the peculiar position of the English towns under New Netherland, in consequence of the war between Holland and England, and of alarming reports in relation to the designs of the Indians, the result whereof was the following:

Convention

Holden at New Amsterdam, to devise and recommend measures for the public security, and to put a stop to the Piracies and Robberies of one Thomas Baxter.

1653 Nov. 26. Johannes La Montagne,
Cornelis van Werckhoven, *from the Council.*
Martin Cregier,
Paulus Leendertsen van der Grist, *from the Burgomasters and Schepens of New Amsterdam.*
George Baxter,
James Hubbard, *Gravesend.*

1653 Nov. 26. John Hicks,
Tobias Feaks, *Flushing.*
Robert Coe,
Thomas Hazard, *Newtown.*
1653 Nov. 27. Another Session was held this day, but Messrs. La Montagne and Werckhoven did not attend it, as the English delegates refused, on the previous day, to acknowledge their right to sit.

Convention

Holden at New Amsterdam to represent the State of the Country to the Anthorities in Holland.

1653 Dec. 10. Arent van Hattem,
Martin Cregier,
Paulus L. van der Grist,
William Beeckman,
Peter Wolfertsen van Couwenhoven, *from the Burgomasters and Schepens New Amsterdam.*
George Baxter,
James Hubbard, *Gravesend.*
John Hicks,
Tobias Feaks, *Flushing.*

1653 Dec. 10. Robert Coe,
Thomas Hazard, *Newtown.*
William Wasborn,
John Somers, *Hempstead.*
Thomas Spycer,
Elbert Elbertsen (Stoothof), *Amersfort.*
Frederick Lubbertsen,
Paulus van der Beecq, *Breuckelen.*
Thomas Swartwout,
Jan Strycker, *Midwout.*

Convention

Holden at New Amsterdam to engage the several Dutch Towns to keep up an armed force for public protection.

1663 July 6. Burgomaster Van der Grist,
Schepen Strycker, *N. Amsterdam.*
Simon Jansen van Aertsdalen,
Roelof Martensen, *Amersfoort.*
William Wilkins,
Charles Morgan, *Gravesend.*

Frederick Lubbertsen,
Peter Pietersen van Nes, *Breuckelen.*
Jan Stryker,
Hendrick Jorissen, *Midwout.*
Rutger Joosten,
Jacob Pietersen, *New Utrecht.*

LANDTS VERGADERING,

Or Meeting of Magistrates of the several Dutch Towns, holden at New Amsterdam, at which the towns mentioned below were represented, but we have the names only of those from two places.

1663 Nov. 3. Paulus Leendertsen van der Grist
Jacob Kip, *New Amsterdam.*

Amersfoort.

Breuckelen.

1663 Nov. 3. *Midwout.*

Harlem.

N. Utrecht.

Ryckous Leydecker,
Guysbert Teunissen, *Boswyck.*

Bergen.

CONVENTION

Holden at Midwout L. I., for the purpose of sending a delegation to Holland, to lay before the States General and West India Company the distressed State of the Country.

1664 Feb. 27. Adriaen Hegeman, *Schout,*
Elbert Elbertsen (Stoothof),
Pieter Claessen,
Roeloff Martensen (Schenck),
Amersfoort,
William Bredenbent,
Albert Cornelissen Wantenaar,

Teunis Gysbertsen Bogaert,
Thomas Verdonck, *Breuckelen.*
William Jacobsen van Boerum,
Hendrick Jorissen,
Jan Snedicker, *Midwout.*
Jacob Pietersen,
Balthazar Vosch,
Francis de Bruyn, *New Utrecht.*
Peter Jansen de Witt,
Barent Joosten, *Boswyck.*

1664 March. Delegates from the English Towns on Long Island assembled at Hempstead this month, with Captain John Scott styled "President," for the purpose of concluding a Treaty with Director Stuyvesant for the Separation of those Towns from New Netherland. We have not the names of the Delegates.

General Assembly

Holden at the City Hall, New Amsterdam.

1664 April 10. Cornelis Steenwyck,
Jacob Backer, *New Amsterdam.*
Jeremias van Renselaer, *President*
Dirck van Schelluyne, *Renselaerswyck.*
Jan Verbeeck,
Gerrit Slechtenhorst, *Fort Orange*
Thomas Chambers,
Gysbert van Imbroch, *Wiltwyck.*
Daniel Terneur,
Johannis Verveelen, *Haerlem.*
David de Marest,
Pierre Billou, *Staten Island.*
William Bredenbent,
Albert Cornelissen Wantenaar, *Breuckelen.*
Jan Strycker,
William Guilliamsen, *Midwout.*
Elbert Elbertsen (Stoothof),
Coert Stevensen (van Voorhees), *Amersfoort.*

1664 April 10. David Jochemsen,
Cornelis Beeckman, *New Utrecht.*
Jan van Cleef,
Gysbert Teunissen (Bogaert), *Boswyck.*
Engelbert Steenhuysen,
Herman Smeeman, *Bergen.*

Convention

Holden at New Orange of Delegates from the Eastern Towns on Long Island, to confer with the Dutch Commanders.

1673.
Thomas James, *Easthampton.*
John Jessup,
Joseph Reynir, *Southampton.*
Thomas Hutchinson,
Isaac Arnold, *Southold.*
Richard Woodhull,
Andrew Miller, *Brookhaven.*
Isaac Platt,
Thomas Skidmore, *Huntington.*

CONVENTION

Holden at New Orange of Delegates from the Dutch Towns to confer with Governor Colve.

1674 Mar. 26. Burgomasters, *New Orange.*
Jacob Strycker, *Long Island.*
Tunis Gysbertse Bogaert,
Jeronimus Rapalie, *Breuckelen.*
Roeloff Martense (Schenck),
Koert Stevensen (van Voorhees), *Amersfoort.*
Jan Stryker,
Auke Jansen, *Midwout.*
Joost Kockuyt,
Hendrick Barentsen Smit, *Bushwyck.*
Hendrick Mattysen Smack,
Cryn Jansen, *New Utrecht.*
Claes Barentse,
Caspar Steynmits, *Bergen.*
Francis Bloodgood, *from the Dutch inhabitants of Flushing, Rustdorp, Middleburgh and Hemstede.*

COMMISSIONERS

To Collect moneys due to the West India Company in New Netherland.

1648 April 17. Lubertus van Dincklage,
Johannes de La Montagne.

To Settle affairs on the South, or Delaware river.

1648 June 7. Lubertus van Dincklage,
Johannes de La Montagne.
1656 May 3. Nicasius de Sille,
Cornelis van Tienhoven.
1659 Sept 23. Cornelis van Ruyven,
Martin Cregier.

To Investigate the Charges against Adriaen van der Donck.

1649 Mar. 5. Paulus Leendertsen van der Grist
Adriaen d'Keyser.

COMMISSIONERS to agree on a Boundary between New Netherland and New England.

1650 Sept. 19. Thomas Willett,
George Baxter.
1663 Oct. 13. Cornelis van Ruyven,
Oloff Stevensen van Cortland,
John Lawrence.

To oblige the Colonie of Rensselaerswyck to publish a certain Ordinance of the Director and Council of New Netherland, and to enforce the execution thereof.

1653 Mar. 28. Cornelis van Tienhoven,
Paulus Leendertsen van der Grist
Maximilian van Gheel,
Johannes Dyckman, and
Two Magistrates of Fort Orange.

To attend the Investigation of an alleged Conspiracy of the Dutch and Indians against the English.

1653 May 23. Johannes de La Montagne,
David Provoost,
Govert Loockermans.

COMMISSIONERS to Superintend the Fortifying of New Amsterdam.

1654 June 16. Nicasius de Sille,
　　　　　　　Arent van Hattem,
　　　　　　　Johannes de La Montagne,
　　　　　　　Martin Cregier,
　　　　　　　Paulus Leendertsen van der Grist
　　　　　　　Peter Wolfertsen van Couwenhoven,
　　　　　　　William Beeckman,
　　　　　　　Oloff Stevensen van Cortland,
　　　　　　　Cornelis van Ruyven.

To Settle the Boundary Line of the Town of Gravesend.

1654 Sept. 3. Paulus Leendertsen van der Grist
　　　　　　　Olof Stevensen van Cortland.
1656 July.　　Nicasius de Sille,
　　　　　　　Cornelis van Tienhoven,
　　　　　　　Thomas Willett.

Commissioners to Erect a Church and Minister's house at Midwout, L. I.

1654 Dec. 17. Rev. Johannes Megapolensis,
Jan Snediger,
Jan Strycker.

To Settle affairs in some of the English Towns on Long Island, and to protest against Encroachments at Oysterbay.

1655 Mar. 16. Johannes de La Montagne,
Cornelis van Tienhoven,
Allard Anthony.

To Treat with the Hackingsack Indians for the release of Christian Prisoners.

1655 Oct. Adrian Post.

To Lay out Streets in the City of New Amsterdam.

1655 Nov. 10. Johannes de La Montagne,
Allard Anthony, and the
Roy Masters.

COMMISSIONERS to Reduce Westchester.

1656 Mar. 7. Frederick de Konick,
Brian Newton,
Cornelis van Tienhoven.

To Settle Affairs at Westchester.

1656. Brian Newton,
Cornelis van Ruyven,
Carel van Brugge.

To Commute for the Tenths of the Crops, or Quit Rents due by the Farmers on Long Island.

1656 July 6. Peter Tonneman,
Gysbert Opdyck.
1658 July 2. Peter Tonneman,
Johan de Deckere.

Commissioners to Settle differences between the Town of Middleburgh (Newtown), L. I., and Thomas Stevenson.

1656 Sept. 22. Johannes de La Montagne,
Thomas Willett.*

To Protect the Town of Flushing against Intrusions of Hempstead, L. I.

1657 June 23. William Lawrence,
Robert Terry,
Tobias Feake.

To Audit the Accounts of Cornelis van Tienhoven.

1657 Mar. 13. Peter Tonneman,
Carel van Brugge,
Matthys Capito.
Mar. 27. Cornelis van Ruyven.

---

* These Commissioners laid out a public Road in the Town, across which Stevenson afterwards ran a fence. This obstruction was ordered to be removed in 1658.

COMMISSIONER to Superintend the ballancing of the Public Accounts.

1658 May 25. Cornelis van Ruyven.

To Treat with the Esopus Indians.

1658.   Martin Cregier,
            Peter Wolphertsen van Couwenhoven,
            Peter Cornelissen van der Veen.
            Augustyn Heermans.

To Purchase the Whorekil, Delaware.

1658.   William Beeckman,
            Alexander d'Hinoyossa.

To Enclose the village of Beverwyck (Albany).

1659 Nov. 4. Francis Boon,
            Dirck Jansen Croon,
            Abraham Staets,
            Adriaen Gerritsen.

NEW NETHERLAND REGISTER. 157

COMMISSIONER to Survey and Enclose Breuckelen and New Utrecht.

1660 Feb. 23. Nicasius de Sille.

To Try persons charged with having murdered an Indian on the Delaware.

1660 Mar. 1. William Beeckman,
Alexander d'Hinoyossa,
Paulus Leendertsen van der Grist
Gerrit van Sweringen,
Jacobus Backer,
Johan Crato,
Nicasius de Sille.

To Lay out, and make a Map of the New Plantations, near Breuckelen.

1660 May 3. Jacques Cortelyou,
Albert Cornelissen (Wantenaar),
Jan Evertsen Bout.

COMMISSIONERS to Enclose the New village at the Esopus.

1661.
Albert Hymanse Roose,
Jan Joosten,
Jan Gerritsen.

To Recover the Christians in the hands of the Esopus Indians.

1663 June.
Johannes de La Montagne,
Johan de Deckere.

To Fortify the village of Bergen.

1663.
Arent Laurens,
Jacob Luby,
Harman Edwards,
Lourens Andriessen,
Paulus Pietersen,
Jan Swaen,
Jan Lubbersen.

Commissioners to Fortify Gemoenepa.

1663 June 18. Gerrit Gerritsen,
Harman Smeeman.
Dirck Claessen.

To Enquire by what Authority certain Persons are attempting to reduce Middleburgh and the neighboring Towns on Long Island, under the English.

1663 Oct. 9. Thomas Willett,
John Laurence,
Cornelis van Ruyven.

To counteract the Mutinous proceedings of Disloyal people in the English Towns on Long Island.

1663 Nov. 6. Nicasius de Sille.

To extinguish the Indian title to the Lands from Barnegatt to the Raritan.

1663 Dec. 6. Martin Cregier,
Govert Loockermans.

COMMISSIONERS to Confer with Captain John Scott, respecting his Claim to Long Island.

1664 Jan 11. Cornelis van Ruyven,
 Oloff Stevensen van Cortland,
 Martin Cregier,
 John Lawrence.

Jan. 12. Cornelis van Ruyven,
 Oloff Stevensen van Cortland,
 Cornelis Steenwyck,
 John Lawrence.

To conclude a Treaty with Captain John Scott for the Cession of the English Towns on the West end of Long Island.

1664 Mar. 3. Oloff Stevensen van Cortland,
 Jacobus Backer,
 John Lawrence, *on the part of the Director General and Council.*
 John Underhill,
 Daniel Denton,
 Adam Mott, *on the part of Captain Scott.*

COMMISSIONERS to Negotiate a Peace between the Mohawks and Abenakis.

1664 May 17. John Davith,
          Jacob Lookermans.

To Ascertain the object of the English fleet below New Amsterdam.

1664 Aug. 29. Johannes de Decker,
          Paulus Leendertsen van der Grist
          Johannes Megapolensis,
          Samuel Megapolensis.

To Confer with Colonel Richard Nicolls.

1664 Sept. 2. Cornelis van Ruyven,
          Cornelis Steenwyck,
          Samuel Megapolensis, M. D.,
          Jacques Cousseau.

Commissioners to Agree on Articles of Capitulation, preliminary to the Surrender of New Netherland to the English.

1664 Sept. 6. Johannes de Decker,
Nicolaes Verlett,
Samuel Megapolensis,
Cornelis Steenwyck,
Oloff Stevensen van Cortland,
Jacques Cousseau.

———

Names signed to the Ratification of the Articles of Capitulation, surrendering New Netherland to the English.

1664 Sept. 8. P. Stuyvesant, *Director General,*
N. de Sille, *Councillor,*
Martin Cregier,
Paulus L. van der Grist, *Burgomaster,*
Peter Tonneman, *Schout,*
Jacob Backer, *President of the Board of Schepens,**
Timotheus Gabry, *Schepen,*

---

* Returned to Holland in 1666.

Isaac Greveraet, *Schepen*,
Nicholas Meyer, *Schepen*.

COMMISSIONERS to the Dutch Commanders on the part of the several Towns in and about the District of Achter-Col, (New Jersey).

1673 Aug. 12. John Baker,
Jacob Melyn,
John Ogden and others.
Aug. 18. John Berry,
William Sandford,
Samuel Edsall,
Laurens Andriessen.

To Confer on behalf of the Burghers of New Orange, with the Dutch Commanders, after the Recovery of New Netherland.

1673 Aug. 14. Cornelis Steenwyck,
Cornelis van Ruyven,
Johannes van Brugh,
Johannes de Peyster,
Martin Cregier,
Nicholas Bayard.

COMMISSIONERS to Administer the Oath of Allegiance to the Inhabitants of the Dutch and English Towns on Long Island, west of Oysterbay.

1673 Aug. 29. William Knyff,
     Jeronimus de Hubert,
     Ephraim Herman.
 Sept. 4. William Laurence,
     Carel van Brugge.

To Administer the Oath of Allegiance to the Inhabitants of the Towns in Achter Col.

1673 Sept. 6. William Knyffe,
     Captain Snel,
     Abram Varlet.

To Administer the Oath of Allegiance to the Inhabitants of the Towns on Long Island, east of Oysterbay.

1673. Oct. 1. William Knyffe,
     Anthony Mallepart,
     Abraham Varlet.
 Oct. 25. William Knyffe,
     Nicolas Vos.

COMMISSIONERS to Value the Houses near Fort Willem Hendrick, New Orange, ordered to be pulled down.

1673 Oct. 10. Cornelis Steenwyck,
  Johannes van Brugh,
  Johannes de Peyster,
  Ægidius Luyck.

To Administer the Oath of Allegiance to the Inhabitants of Southampton, Southold, and Easthampton, L. I.

1673 Oct 30. Cornelis Steenwyck,
  Carel Epestyn,
  Carel Quirynsen.

To Settle the Estate of the late Governor Lovelace.

1673 Nov. 2. Oloff Stevensen van Cortland,
  Gelyn Verplanck,
  Gabriel Minvielle.
Dec. 12. Jacobus van de Water.

COMMISSIONERS to Examine and Settle the Boundary between the Town of New Utrecht and Jan Jansen Veryn's land.

1673 Dec. 5. Cornelis van Ruyven,
      Jacob Strycker.

To Provide Quarters for such of the Outside people as may repair to New Orange in case of being attacked by the English.

1673 Dec. 19. Cornelis Steenwyck,
      Cornelis van Ruyven,
      Johannis van Brugh.

To Administer the Oath of Allegiance to the Inhabitants of Staten Island.

1673 Dec. 21. Carel Epestyn,
      Jan Sol.

To Examine and Report on the Controversy between Roger Townsend and the Town of Westchester.

1673 Dec. 24. William Lawrence,
      Richard Cornwell.

COMMISSIONER to Settle the Estate of Thomas Delaval at Willemstadt.

1674 Jan. 1. Martin Cregier, junr.

To Investigate the Charges against the Schout of Staten Island.

1674 Jan 22. Cornelis van Ruyven,
Carel Epestyn.

To Value the Estates of all persons in New Orange above One thousand Guilders.

1674 Feb. 1. Cornelis Steenwyck,
Nicolas Bayard,
Cornelis van Ruyven,
Oloff Stevensen van Cortland,
Johannes van Brugh,
Ægidius Luyck,
Jacob Kip,
Martin Cregier,
Jacob Leisler,
Francis Rombouts.

1674 Mar. 24. Jacobus van de Water, *Treasurer of the moneys advanced to complete the Fortifications of New Orange, on the Island of Manhattan.*

Commissioners to Examine and Settle the Controversy between Richard Smith and the Town of Huntington, L. I.

1674 Feb. 1. John Laurence,
Richard Cornwell,
Richard Odel,
Thomas Townsend.

To Examine the Books and Audit the Accounts of Cornelis van Ruyven, Receiver of the debts and rents due the West India Company, who is about to return to Fatherland.

1674 June 15. Oloff Stevensen van Cortland,
Gelyn Verplanck,
Gabriel Minvielle,
Jacob van de Water.

COMMISSIONERS to hear and Determine the Differences between the Towns of Piscattaway and Woodbridge, in Achter Col.

1674 June 17. John Lawrence,
  Richard Betts,
  James Hubbert and some Councillors of Achter Col.

To Receive the Books and Accounts of Cornelis van Ruyven, late Receiver, and wind up the affairs of the West India Company.

1674 June 26. Cornelis Steenwyck,
  Nicholas Bayard,
  Jacobus van de Water.

GREAT AND SMALL BURGHERS

OF

NEW AMSTERDAM.

GREAT AND SMALL BURGHERS.

Conferring special privileges on Inhabitants of commercial cities is an offshoot of the Roman Law, whereby it was introduced into Holland, and in time transplanted to New Netherland. Burgher right procured for the citizen Freedom of trade, Exemption from toll and from being sued by a fellow burgher, except in his Burgh. He could not be imprisoned without bail, nor tried for any offense after the lapse of a year. He was saved from attaint and confiscation, if found guilty on a capital charge; for he could not for any crime forfeit more than his life and one hundred guilders. Burgher right by descent or inheritance was gained only through the male line. Females it is true, might be Burghers, but if acquired by purchase, the right was vested in them only whilst Spinsters or Widows. They lost it if they married those not Burghers, but recovered the privilege on decease of such husband. Neither their children nor those of Jewish Burghers inherited the parent's privilege.

In New Netherland, "Great Burghers" only could fill public offices and enjoy exemption from confiscation and attainder, if convicted of a capital offense. All members of the Council, all Burgomasters and Schepens, all Ministers of the Gospel and Commissioned Officers of Militia, past and present, with their descendants in the male line, were declared by this Charter, GREAT Burghers. Others might become such also on payment of the sum of Fifty guilders into the City Treasury.

SMALL Burghers were entitled only to Freedom of trade and to the privilege of being received into their respective Guilds. Natives of the city of New Amsterdam, residents there for a year and six weeks before the date of the Charter, Burghers' sons-in-law, City store keepers, salaried Servants of the Company, and all paying twenty-five guilders, were entitled to have their names inscribed on the roll of SMALL Burghers.

GREAT BURGHERS.

New Amsterdam.

1657.   General Stuyvesant,
April 10. Johannes La Montagne, junr.,
April 11. Jan Gillisen van Bruggh,
    Hendrick Kip,
    Isack Kip,
Aprl. 12. Domine Megapolensis,
   13. Jacob Gerritsen Strycker,
   14. Jan Vinge,
   17. Cornelis Van Tienhoven's Wife,
    Hendrick van Dyck,
    Hendrick Kip, junior,
    Marten Cregier,
April 18. Carel van Bruggh,
    Jacob van Couwenhoven,

1657 April 18. Lourens Cornelisen van Wel,
Johannes Pietersen van Bruggh,
Cornelis Steenwyck,
Wilh. Bogardus,
Daniel Litschoe,
Pieter van Couwenhoven.

SMALL BURGHERS.

1657 April 10. Isack D'Foreest,
Warnaer Wessels,
Nicolaes Langvelthuysen,
April 11. Jan de Jongh,
Jacobus Backer,
Pieter Cornelisen van der Veen,
Pieter Jacobsen Buys,
Abram Nichels,
Pieter Schabanck,
Matheus d'Vos (died in 1663),
Jan Rutgerzen,
Caspar Stynmets,
Pieter Jansen,
Jochem Beeckman, *Shoemaker*,

1657 April 12. Arent Isaacksen, *Shoemaker*,
Fredrick Flipsen, *Carpenter*,
Jacob Mens,
Dirck van Schelluyne.
Cornelis Jansen,
Evert Dirckzen,
Thomas Frerickzen, *Woodsawyers*.
Pieter Caspersen van Naerden,
April 13. Gerrit Pieterzen van Amsterdam,
Hendrick Harmenzen,
Willem Jansen van't Ieverlant,
Hendrick van Bommel, *Tailor*,
David Wessels, *Chairmaker*,
Paulus van der Beeck,
Cornelis Jansen Clopper, *Smith*,
Jean Videt, *Frenchman*,
Gerrit Fullwever,
Lambert Huybertzen Mol,
Michiel Jansen,
Joost Teunizen,
Jacob Clazen Coppe,
Claes Carstensen,

1657 April 13. Ryndert Pieters van Bolsaert,
Andries Hoppen,
Arent Lourizen, *Carpenter*,
Tryntie Hendricksen, widow of Cors Pietersen,
Hendrick Willemzen, *Baker*,
Joost Goderis,
Michiel Pauluzen,
Coenraet Ten Eyck, *Shoemaker*,
Aldert Coninck, *Tailor*,
Rynhout Rynhoutzen, *Shoemaker*,
Pieter Andriezen, *Chimneysweeper*
Jan Jacobsen Carpenel van Haerlem,
Jan Nagel,
Barent Egbertzen, *Tailor*,
1657 April 14. Jan Dirckzen, *Painter*,
Adriaen Vincent,
Isack Teene,
Johannes Beck,
Barent Jacobzen Cool,
Hans Dreper,
Adolph Pieterzen,

1657 April 14. Frerick Arentzen,
Claes Tysen, *Cooper*,
Tosyn Briel,
Sybrant Jansen Galma,
Luycas Dircksen,
Stoffel Elderzen,
Jacob Leunizen,
Hendrick Hendricksen Kip
Sybout Clasen,
Tomas Frans, *Carman*,
Claes Bordingh,
Aryaen Wouterzen,
Symon Felle,
Lodowick Pos,
Jochem Bruynzen,
Tomas Lambertzen, *Carpenter*.
Nicolaes de Meyer,
Evert Duyckingk,
Abram Rycken,
Jan Cornelisen van Hoorn,
Jan Jansen van Ham,
Paulus Heymans,
Tomas Sandersen, *Locksmith*,
Willem Pieterzen d'Groot, senr.,

1657 April 14. Nicolaes d' la Plyne,
Andries Jochemzen,
Jan Hendricksen, *Carpenter*,
Pieter Lourenzen,
Francoys Allard,
Claes van Elslant the elder,
Teunis Tomazen, *Mason*,
Jan Schryver,
Jan Gerritzen, *Mason*,
Jan de Perie,
Abram Pieterzen, *Miller*,
Claes Poulizen,
Cornelis van Langevelt,
Frans Soselje,
Jan Evertsen Bout,
Pieter Jacobs Marius,
Myndert Barentzen,
Jan Cornelissen van Vlensburgh,
Andries Andriezen, from Sweden
Gerrit Jansen Roos, *Carpenter*,
Roelof Jansen, *Mason*,
Jan Hendricksen, *Chairman*,
Jacob Hughes, *Surgeon*,

1657 April 14. Hendrick Pieterzen van Hasselt,
Barent Gerritzen *Tailor*,
Jacob Hendricksen Varvanger,
Pieter Kock,
Matys Capito,
Abram Jacobsen, *Carpenter*,
Aryaen Jansen van Straetkerck,
Luycas Elderzen,
Rynier Gaicheus van Ilst,
Jacob Kalf,
Nicolaes Backer,
Jacob Will van der Bos, *Mason*,
Hendrick Hendricksen, *Drummer*
Claes Pieterzen Kos,
Jacob Leenderzen Vandiegrist,
Jan Cornelissen Buys,
Hendrick Jansen van Scalckwyck,
Jan Lubberzen,
1657 April 17. Resolvert Waldron,
Jan Jansen Hagenaer, *Carpenter*,
Wessel Everts,
Egbert van Borsum,

1657 April 17. Abram Verplanck,
Jan de Pree, *Cooper*,
Geurt Coerten,
Jan Peeck,
Randel Huwit,
Laurens Andries van Boskerck,
Gerrit Gerritzen van Vrieslant,
Tys Lubbertzen,
Abram Lubberzen,
Haey Oelefers,
Jan Pieterzen van Struckhausen,
Corns. Hendricksen,
Rynier Wisselpenningh,
Christaen Barentzen,
Pieter Stoutenberg,
Harman Smeeman,
Egbert Wouterzen,
Leendert Aerden,
Jan Jansen Langedyck,
Andries de Haes,
Claes Tysen van Amsterdam,
Frans Jansen van Brestee, *Cooper*,
Willem Koeck,

1657 April 17. Albert Jansen, *Carpenter*,
Bartel Jansen Roebel,
George Holmes,
Pieter Pieterzen, *Carpenter*,
Hans Kierstede,
Samuel Edsal, *Hatter*,
Frerick Lubbertzen,
Willem Simson, *Englishman*,
Gerrit Cornelissen,
Widow of Jan Huygen,
Jacob Teunizen,
Abram Clock,
Albert Leendertzen,
Jan Hendricksen van Gunst,
Jan Pieterzen, *Miller*,
Nicolaes Verleth,
Herry Breser,
Jacob Walingh,
Borger Jorisen,
1657 April 18. Mettie Wessels,
Jan Jansen van St. Obyn,
Hendrick Arentzen,
Herry Piers,
Jacus Pryn,

1657 April 18. Jacob Stoffelzen,
Andries Clasen, *Tailor*,
Hendrick Jansen van Utrecht,
Claes Pieterzen, *Smith*,
Hendrick Barentzen,
Pelgrom Klock,
Reynier Gerritzen Vries,
Joris van Vorst, *Cooper*,
Willem Claesen, *Butcher*,
Aert Willemsen,
Claes Jansen Ruyter,
Harmen Douwesen,
Hendrick Volckerzen,
Wolfert Gerritsen,
Dirck Claesen, *Pot-baker*,
Juryaen Blanck,
Solomon la Chair,
Claes Jansen van Suermarter,
Frans Claesen,
Huybert Hendricksen van Keulen,
Harman Hendricksen van Deventer, *Shoemaker*.

1657 April 18. Hans Albertzen, *Shoemaker*,
　　　　　　　Carsten Diers van Bremen, *Shoemaker*,
　　April 19. Abram d' la Nooy,
　　　　26. Luycas Andriezen,
　　　　　　Dirck Siecken,
　　　　　　Aryaen Symonzen,
　　　　　　Pieter Rudolphus,
　　　　　　Isack Greveraer,
　　May 3. Jan Hutsitson, *Englishman, ship-carpenter*,
　　　　　Philip Jansen Ringo.

INDEX

Abramse, Cornelis, 100.
Accounts, Commissaries of, 25.
Achter Col, 7, 45, 108, 163, 164, 169.
Achteenhoven, lord of, 7.
Adriaenez v. Duyvelant, Jan 26, 29.
Adriaensen, Joost, 72.
Adriansen, Maryn, 53.
Advocates, 122.
Aerden, Leendert, 181.
Aertsdalen (see *Jansen*).
Agents, Provincial, 136.
Ahasymus, 101.
Albany, 156 (See *Beverwyck ; Fort Orange*).
Albertzen, Hans, 184.
Albrechts, Nicolas, 39.
Allard, Francoys, 179.
Allerton, Isaac, 54.
Alrichs, Israel, 52.
Alrichs, Jacob, 27, 50.
Alrighs, Peter, 47, 51, 52.
Altona, 46, 50, 108.
Amboyna Tragedy, Second, xvi.
Amersfoort, xiii, xvii, 33, 42, 55, 77, 78, 79, 104, 143, 144, 145, 147, 149.
Amsterdam Chamber, Directors of the, 1.
Andriezen, Andries, 179.
Andriessen, Lourens, 158, 163.
Andriezen, Luycas, 184.
Andriezsen, Peter, 177.
Andros, Governor, xx.
Anthony, Allard, 19, 57, 59, 61, 66, 67, 115, 123, 136, 153.
Anthonissen, Cornelis, 133.
Appel, Adrian Jans, 35.
Arentzen Frerick, 178.
Arentzen, Hendrick, 182.
Arnold, Isaac, 45, 148.
Ashman, Robert, 91, 92, 95.

Assembly, first legislative, 140, General, 147.
Attorney General, 38.
Auctioneers (See *Vendue Masters*).
Audit, Board of, 25.
Backer, Jacobus, 63, 64, 136, 138, 147, 160, 162, 175.
Backer, Nicolaes, 180, (See *Willemsen*.)
Backerus, Joannes, 118.
Baeck, Anthony Lodewycksen, 112.
Baker, John, 163.
Bakers, Overseers of, 135.
Baltimore, lord, xix.
Bamboes, Harmen Jacobsen, 34.
Baptists, xviii, 44.
Barens, Joshua, 96.
Barentsen, Christiaen, 113, 181.
Barentse, Claes, 149.
Barents, Frederick, 135.
Barentzen, Hendrick, 183 (See *Smit*)
Barentzen, Myndert, 179.
Barentsen, Peter, 47.
Barentse, Tys, 99.
Barker, John, 98.
Barnegatt, 159.
Barry's court, 125.
Bartels, Jonas, 36, 113.
Bassett, Robert, 121.
Bastiaensen, Michael, 99.
Bastiaensen, Peter, 112.
Baxter, George, 28, 54, 82, 83, 141, 142, 151.
Baxter, Thomas, 141.
Bayard, Balthazar, 29, 100, 107.
Bayard, Nicolas, 23, 24, 27, 28, 29, 32, 103, 114, 163, 167.
Bayles, John, 95.
Bayley, Elias, 43, 110.
Bayley, Nicholas, 98, 121.

Beck, Johannes, 177.
Beck, Jan Juriansen, 50, 51, 108, 131.
Beeckman, Cornelis, 148.
Beeckman, Jochem, 175.
Beeckman, William, 40, 46, 48, 51, 57, 60, 61, 62, 64, 66, 142, 152, 156.
Beer barrels, Inspectors of, 116.
Beeren Island fortified, xiv.
Benckes, Jacob, 10, 22.
Benedict, Thomas, 94.
Bentyn, Jacques, 12, 13, 38, 52.
Bergen, xviii, xix, 46, 100, 107, 110, 117, 133, 145, 148, 149, 158.
Bergen, Martin Gerritsen van, 12.
Berry, John, 163.
Betts, Richard, 86, 87,88, 169.
Betts, William, 98.
Beverwyck, xiv, xvi, 156.
Bibles imported, xvi, and sold by auction, xvii.
Bicker, Gerrit, 50.
Bierman, Henrick, 34.
Biljou, Peter, 45, 99, 107, 147.
Bingson, Mathys, 46.
Blanck, Juryaen, 183.
Bleeker, Jan Jansen, 134.
Block, Adrian, xi.
Blom, Hermanus, 119.
Blomfield, William, 87.
Blommert, Adriaen, 62.
Blommaert, Samuel, 7.
Bloodgood, Francis, 45, 90, 149.
Boerum, William Jacobse van 76, 77, 146.
Boes, Nicolaes, 23.
Bogaert, Gysbert Teunissen, 148.
Bogaert, Harmen Myndertsz van der 30, 48, 124.
Bogaert, Teunis Gysbertse, 75, 146, 149. (See *Guisbert ; Teunissen.*)
Bogardus, Everardus, xv, 118, 128.
Bogardus, Peter, 71.
Bogardus, William, 25, 29, 175.
Bol, Jan Claesen, 16.
Boman, Nicholas, 102.
Bommel, Hendrick van 176.
Bond, Robert, 101.
Bontemantel, Hans, 3, 4, 5.
Book-keepers, 25.
Boon, Francis, 69, 70, 109, 156.
Bordingh, Claes, 178.
Borsum, Egbert van, 117, 180.

Borsum, Hendrick van, 135.
Borsum, Sara van, 134.
Bos, Jacob Will. van der 180.
Boskerck, Lourens Andries van 181.
Boston, 10.
Boswyck, xix, 42, 43, 81, 104, 132, 145, 146, 148, 149.
Bouchesne, Mathys, 111.
Boundary, 151, 152.
Bout, Jan Evertsen, 15, 53, 54, 56, 57, 73, 133, 136, 157, 179.
Bout, William, 37.
Bowne, John, xix.
Bowne, William, 82, 83, 84.
Boyer, Alexander, 49.
Bradish, James, 105.
Braey, Gysbert, 51.
Bread, Inspectors of, 116.
Bredenbent, William, 39, 73, 74, 75, 145, 147.
Bremen, Cartsen Diers van, 184.
Breser, Herry, 182.
Bressani, Joseph, 122.
Bresteede,Hendrick Jansen van,113.
Breuckelen, xiv, xvii, xix, 33, 42, 43, 52, 55, 73, 104, 110, 119, 143, 144, 146, 147, 149, 157.
Brewster, Nathaniel, 106.
Briel, Tousyn, 178.
Broersen, Jan 73.
Brookhaven, 148.
Brooklyn. (See *Breuckelen.*)
Brouse, Edward, 83.
Brouwer, Jan Jans, 11, 12.
Browne, John, 108.
Brudenell, Richard 34.
Brugge. (See *Van Brugge*).
Bruynzen, Jochem, 178.
Burgh, Coenraet, 4, 6.
Burgher provost, 112.
Burgher right, what, 173.
Burghers, Great and Small, 176.
Burgomasters and Schepens, 58.
Burhans, Jan, 72.
Burroughs, John, 87, 105.
Burying ground, 131.
Bushwick. (See *Boswyck*).
Busset, John, 99.
Buys, Jan Cornelissen, 180.
Buys, Pieter Jacobsen, 175.
Bylvelt, Peter, 11.

INDEX.

Campanius, John, 121.
Canada, trade with opened, xviii, 139
Capito, Matthys, 26, 27, 31, 40, 104, 155, 180.
Carelse, Joost, 130.
Carpenel, Jan Jacobsen, 177.
Carpenter, John, 95.
Carpenters, Overseers of, 135.
Cartensen, Claes, 133, 176.
Cassie, Philip, 96.
Casteleyn, Anthony, 6.
Catjouw, Jan, 81.
Catholics, 122.
Cattle arrive in N. Netherland, xii.
Cattskill, xiv, xv.
Chambers, Thomas, 72, 147.
Chaumonot, Peter J. M., 122.
Chichester, James, 95.
Christiaensen, Hendrick, 47.
Christman, Andries Johannes, 28.
Churches, xii, xiii, xiv, xviii, 153.
Clasen, Andries, 183.
Claessen, Dirck, 97, 159, 183.
Claessen, Frans, 131, 183.
Claessen, Peter, 78, 79, 145.
Clasen, Sibout, 178.
Claessen, Valentine, 99.
Claessen, William 103, 183.
Clark, James, 127.
Claverack, xv.
Clergymen, xii, xiii, xvii, xlx, 118.
Clerk, Cornelis, 5.
Clerks in Secretary's office, 28.
Clock, Abram, 182.
Clock, Abraham Martins, 117.
Clock, M. Cornelis, 126.
Clock, Pelgrom, 123, 183.
Cloeck, Peter, 6.
Clopper, Cornelis Jansen, 176.
Cobes, Ludovicus, 110, 123.
Cochrane, John, 87.
Cock, Peter, 102, 180.
Coe, Benjamin, 93.
Coe, Dirck Dircksen, 133.
Coe, John, 86, 87, 88.
Coe, Mr., 91, 94.
Coe, Robert, 85, 94, 106, 142, 143.
Cole, Lanaert, 28.
Coles, Nathaniel, 95.
Coenraatsen, Cornelis, 19.
Coerten, Geurt, 181.
Colendonk, xiv, 8.

Colve, Anthony, 23.
Commissaries, of Accounts, 25: of Districts, 47; of Imports and Exports, what, 31; of Stores, 30.
Commissioners, 150.
Commonalty, Representatives of the, 52.
Communipa, xviii. (See *Gemoenepa*)
Comptroller, 25; of the Windmill, 25
Coney Island, xix.
Coninck, Aldert, 177.
Connecticut, 49, 84, 87, 88, 92, 95, 111, 139.
Consoler of the sick, 129.
Conspiracy against the English, alleged, 151.
Conventions, 140.
Cooke, John, 43, 83, 84.
Cool, Barent Jacobzen, 177.
Coopers, Overseers of, 135.
Coorn, Nicolas, 40.
Coppe, Jacob Clasen, 176.
Corlaer, Arent van, 104. (See *Curler*)
Cornelis, Immetje, 127.
Cornelissen, Adriaen, 97.
Cornelissen, Gerrit, 182.
Cornelissen, Jan, 130, 179. (See *Van Hoorn*).
Cornelissen, Peter, 57, 73, 79, 117, 135.
Cornelissen v. Flensburgh, Sybrant, 126.
Cornwell, Richard, 166, 168.
Corssen, Arent, 49.
Corteljou, Jacques, 37, 41, 114, 157.
Cortland, Oloff Stevensen van, 14, 21, 30, 54, 56, 59, 60, 61, 66, 67, 151, 152, 160, 162, 165, 167, 168.
Cortland, Steven van, 64.
Council, Members of the, 11.
Courber, Wharimus van, 133.
Court, President of the, 24.
Court messengers, 109.
Cousseau, Jacques, 63, 161, 162.
Custurier, Henry, 52.
Couwenhoven, Gerrit Wolphertsen van, 54.
Couwenhoven, Jacob W. van, 55, 56, 136, 174.
Couwenhoven, Peter W. van, 37, 61, 62, 63, 64, 65, 66, 67, 115, 133, 142, 152, 156, 175.
Couwenhoven, W. Gerritsen van, 75.

INDEX.

Crabbe, Jacob, 102.
Crane, Jasper, 101.
Crato, Jan, 52.
Cregier, Martin, 19, 21, 58, 59, 60, 66, 67, 113, 137, 141, 142, 150, 152, 156, 159, 160, 162, 163, 167, 174.
Cregier, Martin, junr., 26, 27, 28, 167.
Cresson, Peter, 96.
Crol, Bastiaen Jansen, 47.
Cromwell, Oliver, xviii.
Croon, Dirck Jansen, 68, 69.
Crynen, Dirck, 111, 112.
Curacao, 15, 29.
Curler, Jacobus van, 12, 13, 30, 49, 57, 80, 105, 115, 131.
Curtius, Alexander Carolus, 126, 131
Dablon, Claude, 122.
Dam, Jan Jansen, 52, 54, 55.
Daniels, Jan, 39, 46.
David, Jan, 134, 161.
De Beauvois, Carel, 110, 132.
De Bleuw, Francis, 136.
De Bruyn, Francis, 80, 105, 114, 146.
Decker, Johannes de, 20, 21, 22, 25, 48, 123, 138, 154, 158, 161, 162.
De Foreest, Isaac, 33, 34, 35, 57, 62, 116, 175.
De Fries, Jan, 14.
De Graeff, Cornelis, 6.
De Groot, Gerrit, 111.
De Groot, Jacob Pietersen, 97.
De Groot, Willem Pietersen, 178.
De Haes, Andries, 181.
De Haes, Roelof Jansen, 24.
De Hooges, Anthony, 104.
De Key, William, 22, 28.
De la Nooy, Abram, 184.
Delavall, Thomas, 167.
Delaware river, 8, 27, 46, 47, 49, 102, 123, 127, 150, 156.
DeLeeuw, Gysbert, 14.
De Marest, David, 97, 99, 147.
De Meyer, Nicolaes, 178.
De Milt, Anthony, 41.
Denton, Daniel, 94, 102, 105, 106, 160.
Denton, Nathaniel, 93, 94, 95, 106.
Denton, Richard, 120.
De Peyster, Johannes, 60, 61, 62, 63, 66, 67, 163, 165.
De Potter, Cornelis, 122.
De Pree, Jan, 181.
Deputy Provincial Secretaries, 28.

Dormer, Captain Thomas, xi.
Deventer, Jan van, 81. (See *Hendricksen.*)
De Vos, Mattheus, 110, 123, 175.
De Vries, David Pietersen, 52.
De Witt, Jan, 117.
De Witt, Peter Jansen, 81, 146.
De Witt, Tierck Claessen, 72.
Dincklage, Lubertus van, xv, 12, 15, 16, 17, 18, 24, 115, 150.
Dincklage, Margaretta van, 17.
Dircksen, Adriaen, 31, 47.
Dircksen, Barent, 54.
Dircksen, Evert, 176.
Dircksen, Gerrit, 53.
Dircksen, Jan, 135, 177.
Dircksen, Joris, 73, 74.
Dircksen, Luycas, 178.
Dircksen, Lysbet, 128.
Dirckse, Volckert, 82.
Directors of Amsterdam Chamber,1.
Directors General, 9.
Disbrow, Henry, 99.
Douty, Francis, 54, 120.
Douwesen, Harmen, 134, 183.
Draeyer, Andrew, 40, 48.
Dreper, Hans, 177.
Drisius, Samuel, xvi, 118, 138.
Du Bois, Louis, 72.
Du Parck, Jan, 126.
Duperon, Francis, 122.
Duyckinck, Evert, 31, 113, 178.
Duyster, Dirck Cornelissen, 47.
Duyvelant. (See *Adriaensz*).
Dyckman, Hugh, 101.
Dyckman, Joannes, 25, 48, 151.
Earthquake, xix.
Eastchester, 98.
Easthampton, 96, 107, 148, 165.
Ebbingh, Jeronimus, 62, 63, 64.
Ebel, Peter, 111, 134.
Edsall, Samuel, 163, 182.
Edwards, Harman, 158.
Eelkins, Jacob, 47.
Egbertzen, Barent, 177.
Eight Men, the, 48.
Elbertsen, Elbert. (See *Stoothof*).
Eldersen, Hendrick, 31.
Elderzen, Luycas, 180.
Elderzen, Stoffel, 178.
Elizabethtown, 45, 101.
Elslant, Claes van, 12, 30, 109, 115, 179.

INDEX.   189

Emans, John, 85.
Engelbrecht, Jan, 135.
English, New Netherland usurped by the, 10.
English Secretaries, 28.
Ennesen, Barent, 136.
Epesteyn, Carel, 165, 166, 167.
Esopus, xvi, xvii, xix, 21, 27, 40, 48, 57, 59, 60, 64, 104, 126, 128, 132, 156, 158.
Everett, Richard, 93.
Everts, Cornelis, 10, 22, 37.
Everts, Wessel, 180.
Excise Law introduced, xiv; referred to, 33, 34, 35.
Fairs established, xv.
Farmers of the Revenue, 33.
Farrington, Edward, 88, 89.
Feake, Henry, 85, 86.
Feake, Tobias, 42, 142, 155.
Felle, Symon, 178.
Ferman, Robert, 95.
Ferry masters, 117.
Fire Island, ship wrecked at, xviii.
Firewardens, 113.
Fiscal. (See *Schout-Fiscals*).
Fish, Jonathan, 86.
Fisher Edward, 105.
Five Dutch Towns, the, 42, 105, 114.
Five English Towns, 45, 106.
Flatbush, xvi. (See *Midwout*).
Flatlands, xiii. (See *Amersfoort*).
Flipsen, Fredrick, 176.
Flushing, xiv, xvii, 27, 36, 42, 45, 88, 105, 106, 110, 120, 142, 149, 155.
Folcks ——— 127.
Fordham, 99, 107.
Fordham, Josiah, 120.
Fordham, Robert, 120.
Forman, Robert, 92. (See *Ferman*).
Fort Amsterdam completed, xiii.
Fort Casimir, xvi, xvii, 4, 6, 50, 51, 108.
Fort Christina, xiii, 121.
Fort Good Hope, xii, xvi, 49, 139.
Fort Nassau, near Albany, xi.
Fort Nassau (N. J.), xii, 47, 48, 49.
Fort Orange, xii, xiv, xviii, 20, 33, 34, 35, 36, 37, 39, 47, 67, 68, 103, 109, 110, 119, 126, 132, 147, 151. (See *Beverwyck*.)
Fort Trinity, xvii.

Frans. Thomas, 178.
Fredericks, Thomas, 100, 176.
Fremin, Jacques, 122.
Fullwever, Gerrit, 176.
Gabry, Timotheus, 63, 64, 103, 114, 162.
Gaicheus van Ilst, Rynier, 180.
Galma, Sybrant Jansen, 178.
Gangeloffsen, Claes, 113.
Geelvinck, Cornelis, 6.
Geerts, Tryntie, 134.
Gemoenepa, 100, 159.
Gerritsen, Adriaen, 69, 70, 156.
Gerritsen, Barent, 180.
Gerritsen, Gerrit, 100, 159, 181.
Gerritsen, Goosen, 70. (See *Van Schaack*).
Gerritsen, Jan, 158, 179.
Gerrits, Otto, 37.
Gerritsen, Philip, 117.
Gerritsen, Wolfert, 183.
Gezel, Cornelis van, 51, 52, 108.
Gezel, Hendrick Gerritsen van, 111.
Gibbons, Richard, 43.
Gilbert, Josias, 98.
Gilder, Johannes van, 131.
Gildersleeve, Richard, 85, 90, 91, 92.
Glen, Sander Leenderstsen, 68, 69, 70, 71.
Goderis, Joost, 177.
Godyn, Samuel, 7.
Goetwasser, Joannes Ernestus, 121.
Goulding, William, 105.
Grace, George, 139.
Grain measurers, 116.
Grasmeer, Wilhelmus, 119.
Gravesend, xiii, xiv, xvii, 42, 43, 82, 105, 140, 141, 142, 143, 152.
Grevenraet, Isaac, 40, 63, 64, 163, 184.
Guiljamsen, William, 77, 147. (See *Willemse*).
Guisbert, Teunis, 79. (See *Bogaert*).
Gunst, Jan Hendricksen van, 182.
Gysbertsen, Albert, 72. (See *Meteren*)
Hackingsack, 153.
Haen, Laurens, 30.
Haes. (See *De Haes*).
Hagenaer, Jan Jansen, 180.
Hainelle, Michel, 104.
Hall, Thomas, 54, 56, 113.
Hallet, William, xviii, 44, 90.

INDEX.

Hamel, —— 104.
Hanius, Joannes, 17.
Hanoe, John, 101.
Hanout, B, 104.
Hansen, Laurens, 133.
Hansen, Matys, 102.
Harck, William, 44.
Hardenbergh, Arnoldus van, 55, 56.
Hardenbrook, Adolph, 100.
Harlem, xix, 41, 96, 103, 132, 145, 147.
Harling, Jan Pietersen, 97.
Harmenzen, Hendrick, 176.
Harmensen, Reynert, 11.
Hart, Edward, 36, 105.
Hartford, xvi, 9.
Hartgers, Peter, 68, 69.
Harvey, Mathias, 100.
Hatem, Arent van, 57, 58, 59, 135, 142, 152.
Hawthorne, William, 139.
Hays, William, 125.
Hazard, Jonathan, 88.
Hazard, Thomas, 85, 142, 143.
Heerman, Augustyn, 55, 56, 137, 138, 156.
Hegeman, Adriaen, 42, 76, 104, 132, 145.
Hegeman, Peter, 42.
Hellakens, Jacob, 80.
Hempstead, xiv, 34, 44, 45, 90, 105, 106, 110, 120, 140, 143, 146, 149, 155.
Hendricksen, Corns., 181.
Hendricksen, Frederick, 135.
Hendricks, Gerrit, 34, 35, 36, 37.
Hendricksen van Deventer, Harmen, 183.
Hendricksen, Hendrick, 180.
Hendricksen van Keulen, Huybert, 183.
Hendricksen, Jan, 102, 133, 179. (See *Deventer*).
Hendricksen, Roeloff, 72.
Hendrickzen, Tryntie, 177.
Herbertsen, Andries, 68, 69, 70.
Herder, Peter Petersen, 52, 102.
Hermans, Arent, 97.
Herman, Ephraim, 29, 103, 164.
Hervey, Jan, 126.
Hesse, Jacob Jansen, 12.
Heymans, Albert 71.
Heymans, Paulus, 134, 178.
Hicks, John, 44, 88, 90, 91, 92, 142.
Hill, Mr. 139.

Hinchman, John, 90.
Hinojossa, Alexander d', 48, 51, 156.
Hinse, Jacob d', 126.
Hoboken, xvii.
Hoboken, Harmen van, 131.
Hoit, John, 98.
Holdsworth, Jonas, 106.
Holmes, George, 116, 182.
Homs, Samuel, 85.
Hooft, Hendrick, 6.
Hoogeboom, Cornelis, 72.
Hooghteling, Jan Willemsen, 72.
Hooglant, Christoffel, 64, 116.
Hoogland, Cornelis Dircksen, 117.
Hopkins, Samuel, 101, 108.
Hopman, Hans, 51.
Hoppen, Andries, 177.
Hospital, Matron of the, 128; first on Manhattan island, 128.
Houten, Hans Jorissen, 47.
Houthuysen, Dirck, 136.
Howell, Edward, 96.
Hubbard, James, 43, 82, 83, 84, 141, 142, 169.
Hubert, Jeronimus de, 164.
Hudde, Andries, 12, 27, 30, 37, 46, 49, 50, 51, 108, 130.
Hudson, Henry, discovers New Netherland, v, vi.
Hudson river, first English at, xii; declared free, xvi.
Huesden, Laurens van, 31.
Huestis, Robert, 98.
Hugues, Jacobus, 126, 179.
Hunt, Ralph, 86, 87, 88.
Huntington, 45, 107, 148, 168.
Hurley, 72.
Hutchinson, Thomas, 96, 148.
Hutsitson, Jan, 184.
Hewit, Randel, 181.
Huyghens, Cornelis van der, 13, 14, 15, 38.
Huyghens, Hendrick, 50.
Huyghen, Jan, 30, 182.
Ilpendam, Adrian, 130.
Ilpendam, Jan Jansen van, 49.
Imbroch, Gysbert van, 72, 126, 147.
Independents, 120.
Indian Interpreters, 133.
Indians, 153, 156, 158.
Influenza, xv.
Inspection laws introduced, xiii.

INDEX. - 191

Inspectors, 115.
Isaacksen, Arent, 176.
Jacobsen, Abram, 180.
Jacobsen van Schagen, Claes, 134.
Jacobsen, Rutger, 68, 70.
Jacobs, William, 93.
Jacobse, Walinck, 100.
Jackson, Robert, 92, 93.
Jacquet, Jean Paul, 50, 113.
Jailer, 112.
Jamaica, (L. I.), 44, 45. (See *Rystdorp*).
James, John, 105, 106.
James, Thomas, 148.
Jans, Annetje, 128.
Jansen, Albert, 182.
Jansen, Adriaen, 35.
Jansen, Andries, 132.
Jansen, Anthony, 110.
Jansen van Vlieringen, Arent, 111.
Jansen, Arian, 130, 180.
Jans, Auke, 78, 149.
Janse, Barent, 71.
Jansen, Claes, 101.
Jansen, Cornelis, 176.
Jansen, Cryn, 149.
Jansen van Brestee, Frans, 181.
Jansen, Foppe, 32.
Jansen, Hendrick, 13, 53,113,180,183
Jansen, Isaac, 125.
Jansen van Noorstrande, Jacob, 116
Jansen de Jongh, Jan, 113.
Jansen, Marcelis, 33, 35.
Jansen van Breuckelen, Martin, 78.
Jansen, Maurits, 30, 31.
Jansen, Michael, 56, 100, 116, 176.
Jansen, Paulus, 50, 51.
Jansen, Peter, 135, 175.
Jansen, Rem, 76.
Jansen, Roeloff, 36, 179.
Jansen van Aertsdalen, Simon, 79, 143.
Jansen, Stoffel, 71.
Jansen, Teunis, 75.
Jansen, Thomas, 81.
Jansen, Tryn, 128.
Jansen, Tymen, 135.
Jansen, Volckert, 68.
Jansen, William, 117, 176.
Jessup, Edward, 86, 98.
Jessup, John, 148.
Jesuits, xviii.

Jochemzen, Andries, 179.
Jochimsen, David, 81, 148.
Jochemsen, Hendrick, 72.
Jogues, Isaac, xiii, xiv, 122.
Jongh, Jan de, 175.
Joosten, Barent, 81, 146.
Joosten, Bores, 102.
Joosten, Jan, 73, 158.
Joosten Rutger, 144.
Joosten, Simon, 109, 110.
Joris, Adriaen, 9.
Joris, Hellegonda, 120.
Jorissen, Abram, 80.
Jorissen, Borger, 182.
Jorissen, Hendrick, 77, 78, 144, 146.
Juriaensen, Barent, 85.
Kalf, Jacob, 180.
Keulen. (See *Hendricksen*).
Keyser, Adrian, 16, 17, 18, 25, 26, 27, 113, 114, 137, 150.
Kieft, William, 9, 15, 16, 53.
Kierstede, Hans, 124, 125, 182.
Kierstede, Roeloff, 72.
Kierstede, Sara, 134.
Kings county, 42.
Kingston. (See *Wiltwyck*).
Kip, Hendrick, 55, 56, 62, 102, 113, 115, 174, 178.
Kip, Isaac, 174.
Kip, Jacob, 27, 28, 62, 63, 64, 103, 144, 167.
Kleyn, Elmerhuysen, 51, 52.
Klock. (See *Clock*).
Knyff, William, 23, 38, 164.
Kock. (See *Cock*).
Kockuyt, Joost, 149.
Kocx, Gerrit, 33.
Koeck, Willem, 181.
Konick, Frederick de, 154.
Kos, Claes Pietersen, 180.
Kreeckenbeck, Daniel, 47.
Krol, Bastiaen Jansen, 14.
Kuyter, Jochim Pietersen, xv, 13, 41, 57, 61.
Labadie, Jean, 47.
Laborers, Overseers of, 134.
Lachair, Solomon, 34, 35, 123, 183.
La Grange, Joost de, 50, 102.
Lake Champlain discovered, xi.
Lake George discovered, xiv.
Lake Ontario discovered, xi.
Lambertzen, Thomas, 178.

192 INDEX.

Lammertse, Thomas, 76.
Lampo, Jan, 11, 12, 38.
Langedyck, Jan Jansen, 181.
Langevelt, Cornelis, 179.
Langvelthuysen, 175.
Latin school, 118, 131.
Laughton, John, 106.
Layton John, 87.
Le Bleu, Francis, 122.
Landts vergadering, 144.
Lantsingh, Hendrick, 134.
Lawrence, John, 105, 151, 159, 160, 168, 169.
Laurence, Thomas, 105,
Lawrence, William, 45, 88, 89, 155, 164, 166.
Laurents, Arent, 158.
Leendertzen, Albert, 182.
Legislative Assembly, first, 140.
Leisler, Jacob, 167.
Le Mercier, Francois, 122.
Le Moyne, Simon, 122, 139.
Lequier, John, 81.
Letcher, Jan, 81.
Le Thor, Johan, 2.
Leunizen, Jacob, 178.
Leverich, William, 120, 127.
Leydecker, Ryck, 81, 145.
Lime measurers, 116.
Litscheo, Daniel, 113, 175.
Lokenius, Laurence Charles, 121.
Long Island, xii, xvi, xvii, xix, xx, 19, 33, 34, 35, 36, 107, 117, 119, 146, 148, 149, 153, 154, 160, 164.
Loockermans, Govert, 55, 56, 57, 62, 63, 67, 113, 133, 151, 159.
Lookermans, Jacob, 161.
Looten, Dirck, 29, 32.
Loper, Jacob, 16.
L'Oragne, Jacob, 124, 126.
Lord, John, 97, 93.
Lott, Peter, 76, 78.
Lourentsen, Andries, 48.
Lourenzen, Pieter, 179.
Lourizen, Arent, 177.
Lovelace, Gov. 165.
Lubberzen, Abram, 181.
Lubbertsen, Frederick, 53, 73, 75, 143, 144, 182.
Lubbertsen, Jan, 29, 131, 158, 180.
Lubbertzen, Tys, 181.
Luby, Jacob, 158.

Ludekens, David, 127.
Lupold, Ulrich, 13, 30, 38.
Lutherans, xvii, xviii, 121.
Lutten, Walraven, 99.
Luyck, Ægidius, 60, 118, 131, 165.
Maelstyn, Sander, 102.
Maenhout, Boudewyn, 132.
Magistrates, 68.
Mallepart, Anthony, 164.
Man, Edward, 2, 3, 4, 6.
Mangnussen, Mangnus, 135.
Manhattan Island, first settlement on, xi: Population of, xii; xvi: mentioned, 52, 55, 168: first Hospital on, 128.
Mamaroneck, 99.
Maps, 157.
Marbletown, 73.
Marcellisen, Peter, 100.
Marcken, Jan Gerritsen, van, 36, 40, 123.
Marius, Pieter Jacobs, 179.
Marlet, Gideon, 99.
Martense, Roeloff, 78, 80. (See *Schenck*).
Marvine, Robert, 106.
Maryland, xix, 138.
Masons, Overseers of, 135.
Massachusetts, xviii, 139.
Mastine, John, 44, 110.
Matthews, Gov., 138.
Mathews, Samuel, 93.
Mattyssen. (See *Smack*).
Measurers of grain and lime, 116.
Megapolensis, Joannes, 118, 119, 153, 161, 174.
Megapolensis, Johannes, junr. 126.
Megapolensis, Samuel, 118, 126, 161, 162.
Melyn, Cornelis, xv, 8, 54.
Melyn, Jacob, 101, 163.
Menard, Rene, 122.
Mens, Jacob, 176.
Messenger, Andrew, 93, 94.
Meteren, Jan Gysbertse van, 81.
Mey, Cornelis Jacobsen, 9.
Meyer, Nicolaus, 64, 163.
Michaelius, Jonas, 118.
Michielsen, Christopher, 112.
Michielse, Elias, 100.
Michielse, Enoch, 100.

INDEX.

Middleburgh, 43, 45, 85, 105, 106, 110, 120, 127, 132, 140, 149, 153, 159. (See *Newtown*).
Middletown, 45.
Midwives, 128.
Midwout, xvii, 33, 42, 76, 79, 119, 132, 143, 144, 145, 146, 147, 149, 153.
Miller, Andrew, 148.
Millers, 117.
Mills, Richard, 107, 120. 132.
Minckaque, 101.
Minuit, Peter, xiii, 9.
Minvielle, Gabriel, 165, 168.
Mol, Lambert Huybertzen, 176.
Molenaar, Arent Evertsen, 133.
Mollenaer, Jacob, 125.
Mollenaer, Thomas, 98.
Montagne, Jesse La, 31.
Montagne, Johannes La, 13, 14, 15, 16, 17, 18, 19, 20, 48, 49, 115, 124, 125, 141, 142, 150, 151, 152, 153, 155, 158, 174.
Montagne, Johannes La, junr., 26, 34, 41, 96, 97, 113.
Montagne, Johannes Momie de La, 130, 132.
Montagne, William La, 104.
Montfoort, Peter, 74.
Moody, Sir Henry, 139.
Moore, John, 120.
More, Thomas, 96.
Morgan, Charles, 42, 143.
Morris, John, 43.
Mott, Adam, 160.
Mulford, John, 96.
Muller, Hendrick, 39.
Muyden, Michel, 97.
Myndertsen, Jan Jansen, 11.
Meyndertsen v. Keren, Meyndert. 7.
Naerden, Pieter Caspersen van, 176.
Nagel, Jan, 177.
Naval officer, 23.
Nederhost, lord of, 7.
Negroes, 134.
Nevesinck, 8.
Nevius, Johannes, 61 103.
New Amstel, xviii, 6, 46, 47, 50, 51, 102, 108, 119, 121, 133.
New Amsterdam, xv, 24, 33, 34, 35, 36, 41, 42, 55, 57, 65, 103, 109, 110, 113, 114, 121, 123, 129, 143, 144, 147, 152, 153, 161, 174.

Newark, 45, 101, 108.
New England, 35, 137, 151.
New Haven, xv, 137.
New Jersey, xiv, xix, 45, 52, 163.
Newman, Thomas, 97, 98.
New Netherland discovered, v, xi; population of, xiv, xx; surrendered, 162.
New Orange, xx, 41, 103, 148, 149, 163, 165, 166, 167, 168.
New Plymouth, trade opened with, xii.
Newton, Brian, 15, 17, 18, 32, 138,154.
Newton, Thomas, 43.
Newtown, xvi, 45, 142, 143, 155. (See *Middleburgh*).
New Utrecht, xiv, xvi, xix, 8, 19, 42, 43, 80, 105, 144, 145, 146, 148, 149, 157, 166.
New Village in the Maizeland, 46.
New York, xx; first glimmer of a representative form of government in, 52.
Nichels, Abraham, 175.
Nicolls, Richard, 161.
Niessen, ensign, 48.
Nine Men, the, 55.
Noble, William, 89, 90, 126.
Noorstrande. (See *Jansen*).
Nooy. (See *De la Nooy*.)
Notaries, 123.
Notelman, Coenraad, 38.
Nyack, (L. I.), xvi, 8.
Nyssen, Teunis, 74, 75.
Oblinis, Joost, 97.
Odel, Richard, 168.
Oelefers, Haey, 131.
Ogden, John, 45, 101, 163.
Oldemarckt, Willem Cornelissen, 14
Onondaga Salt Springs discovered, xvi ; French settle at, xviii.
Oosting, Jan, 127.
Opdyck, Gysbert, 13, 15, 31, 49, 54, 109, 154.
Orphan masters, 65.
Orphans, Matron of, 127.
Oswego, xvi.
Overseers, 134.
Oysterbay, xvii, 45, 95, 106, 111, 153, 164.
Paauw, Michael, 7.
Palmer, Joseph, 98.

194 INDEX.

Palmer, William, 86.
Pampton, Richard, 98.
Pater, A., 2.
Pastoor, Frans Barentsen, 68, 70.
Patroons, 7.
Pauluszoon, Michel, 49, 118, 177.
Pauw, Jan, 125.
Pavonia, xii, xvii, 7, 48, 52, 55.
Peeck, Jan, 181.
Pels, Evert, 71, 72.
Pergens, Jacob, 1, 2, 3, 4, 5.
Perie, Jan de, 179.
Pettit, Thomas, 43.
Philadelphia, xiv.
Philips. (See *Flipsen*.)
Physicians, 124.
Pickes, Vincent, 26.
Piers, Herry, 182.
Pierson, Henry, 107.
Pietersen, Abram, 53, 54, 117, 179.
Pieterzen, Adolph, 177.
Pietersen, Claes, 183.
Pietersen, Cors, 177.
Pietersen, Evert, 131, 133.
Pietersen, Gerrit, 176.
Pietersen, Gillis, 135.
Pietersen, Hendrick, 135, 180.
Pietersen, Jacob, 80, 144.
Pietersen, Jan, 112, 125, 182.
Pietersen, Paulus, 158.
Pieterzen, Pieter, 182.
Pieters, Ryndert, 177.
Pieterzen van Struckhausen, Jan, 181.
Pietersen van Bossaert, William, 135.
Pietersen, Wybrant, 30, 115.
Piscattaway, 45, 102, 169.
Planck, Abram, 53.
Planck, Jacob Albertsen, 39.
Platt, Isaac, 95, 148.
Plowden, Sir Edmund, xiv.
Plyne, Nicolas d' la, 179.
Polhemus, Joh. Theod., 119.
Poncet, Joseph, xvi, 122.
Pos, Lodewyck, 178.
Pos, Simon Dircksen, 11, 12.
Post, Adrian, 153.
Potter, Cornelis de, 78.
Poulizen, Claes, 179.
Powell, Thomas, 107.
Provincial Agents, 136.
Provincial Secretaries, 27.

Provoost, David, 30, 31, 42, 49, 55, 57, 115, 123, 130, 151.
Proovost, Johannes, 25, 32, 103.
Provost marshals, 111.
Pryn, Jacus, 182.
Puritans refused permission to go to New Netherland, xi.
Quakers, xviii, xix, 89, 93.
Quirynsen, Carel, 165.
Quit rents introduced, xiii ; referred to, 154.
Rambo, Peter, 102.
Ramsden, John, 87.
Rapalje, George, 53, 73, 74.
Rapalje, Jan Jorissen, 75.
Rapalie, Jeronimus, 149.
Ragueneau, Paul, 122.
Raritan, xix, 159.
Rasenburgh, William, 127.
Rasieres, Isaac de, 11, 25, 27.
Ravens, R., 108.
Raye, Jehan, 1.
Receiver general, 24.
Religious persecution, xvii.
Remund, Jan van, 27.
Renselaerswyck, xii, xv, xvi, 7, 12, 39, 40, 104, 110, 119, 147, 151.
Representatives of Commonalty, 52.
Revenue, Farmers of the, 32.
Reynir, Joseph, 148.
Reynst, Jacobus, 4.
Rhode Island, 137.
Rhodes, John, 103.
Richards, John, 139.
Rickbell (Rigebell), John, 95, 111.
Ringo, Philip Jansen, 184.
Rodenberch, Johannes, 28.
Roebel, Bartel Jansen, 182.
Roelantsen, Adam, 31, 111, 129.
Roessen, Jan Hendrick, 49.
Roeters, Hendrick, 6.
Rombouts, Francis, 54, 167.
Roos, Gerrit Jansen, 179.
Roosa, Adriaen Albertsen, 72.
Roose, Albert Hymanse, 158.
Root, Simon, 133.
Rossum, Huyg Aertsen van, 73.
Roy masters, 115.
Rudolphus, Pieter, 184.
Rustdorp, xviii, 45, 93, 106, 149. (See *Jamaica*).
Rutgersen, Jan, 175.

INDEX. 195

Ruyter, Claes Jansen, 133, 134, 183.
Ruyven, Cornelis van, 20, 21, 22, 23, 24, 27, 137, 150. 151, 152, 154, 155, 156, 159, 160, 161, 163, 166, 167, 168, 169.
Ruyven, Levinus van, 29.
Ruyven, Peter, 29.
Rycken, Abram, 178.
Ryckhaert, Joannes, 1, 2. 4.
Rynvelt, ——— 127.
Rynevelt, Abraham, 51.
Rynhoutsen, Rynhout, 177.
Ryverdingh, Peter, 103, 110.
St. Obyn, Jan Jansen van, 182.
Salt Springs discovered, xvii.
Sam, Jacob, 26, 32, 33.
Sandersen, Thomas, 178.
Sandford, William, 163.
Saul, Thomas, 88.
Schaefbanck, Peter, 109, 175.
Schaets, Gideon, 119.
Schelluyne, Dirck van, 104, 110, 123. 147, 176.
Schenck, Roeloff Martense, 145, 149.
Schenectady, xix, xx, 40, 71, 123.
Schermerhoorn, Jacob Jansen, 68, 69, 71.
Schoolmasters, xii, 120, 129.
Schools, xix, 55, 118; Greek and Latin, 131.
Schout fiscals, 38; deputy, 39: local, 39.
Schryver, Jan, 179.
Schulenborch, Ferd, 1, 2.
Schut, Gerrit, 125.
Schut, Jan Willemsen, 30.
Schudt, William Jansen, 73.
Schuyler, David, 71.
Schuyler, Philip Pietersen, 68, 69, 70.
Scott, John, xx, 84, 87, 146, 160.
Seaman, John, 90, 91, 93.
Seatalcot, 45, 106, 107.
Secretaries, provincial, 27; deputy, 28; English, 28; clerks of, 28.
Selyns, Henricus, 119.
Shaving not an exclusive appurtenance of chirurgery, 124.
Sheriffs. (See *Schout fiscals*.)
Shrewsbury, 45, 101.
Siecken, Dirck, 184.
Siecken, Jan Dircksen, 101.

Sille, Nicassius de, 18, 19, 20, 21, 22, 29, 38, 43, 150, 152, 157, 159, 162.
Simson, Willem, 182.
Skidmore, Thomas, 148.
Slaughter excise, 34, 37.
Slavery established, xii; slaves imported, xvi.
Slecht, Cornelis Barentsen, 71, 128.
Slechtenhorst, Brant Arent van, 40.
Slechtenhorst, Gerrit van, 40, 71, 147.
Slot, Jan Pietersen, 96, 97.
Smack, Hendrick Mattysen, 81, 149.
Smallpox, xix.
Smally, John, 102.
Smeeman, Herman, 100, 148, 159, 181.
Smith, Dirck, 48, 50.
Smit, Hendrick Barentse, 82, 149.
Smith, John, 93, 98.
Smith, Richard, 54, 168.
Smiths, Overseers of, 136.
Snedicker, Jan, 76, 77, 146.
Snel, Capt., 164.
Sol, Jan, 166.
Somers, John, 143.
Soselje, Frans, 179.
Southampton, 45, 90, 96, 106, 107, 148, 165,.
Southold, 45, 107, 148, 165.
South river, 8, 9, 10, 19, 21, 32, 33, 47. (See *Delaware*.)
Specx, J., 1, 2.
Spicer, Samuel, 84.
Spicer, Thomas, 83, 143.
Spiegel, Dirck, 5.
Staets, Abraham, 69, 70, 126, 156.
Staten island, xii xiii, xvii, 8, 45, 99, 107, 147, 166, 167.
Steenhuysen, Engelbert, 100, 133, 148.
Steenwick, Cornelis, 23, 60, 62, 67, 136, 137, 147, 160, 161, 162, 163, 165, 166, 167, 169, 175.
Steinmits, Caspar, 100, 175.
Stevensen, Coert, 79, 80.
Stevensen, John, 130.
Stevenson, Thomas, 155.
Steyn, Hans, 130.
Steynmits, Claes, 149.
Stickland, John, 91, 94.
Stille, Oloff, 102.
Stillwell, Nicolas, 78, 82, 83.

INDEX.

Stillwell, Richard, 84, 85.
Stirling, Lord, Long island conveyed to, xiii.
Stodder, Tymen, 127.
Stoers, Claes Arentse, 46, 107, 111.
Stoffelsen, Jacob, 15, 30, 53, 54, 134, 183.
Stoothof, Elbert Elbertsen, 56, 78, 79, 80, 143, 145, 147.
Stoutenberg, Peter, 181.
Stretton, John, 96.
Strycker, Jacob, 42, 61, 62, 63, 67, 143, 149, 166.
Strycker, Jacob Geritsen, 174.
Strycker, Jan, 76, 77, 78, 143, 144, 147, 149, 153.
Stuyvesant, Peter, 9, 10, 15, 16, 17, 61, 146, 162, 174.
Suermarter, Claes Jansen van, 183.
Surgeons, 124.
Surveyors general, 37; city, 115.
Swaen, Jan, 158.
Swaenenburgh, xx, 72.
Swanendael, xii, 7.
Swaine, Francis, 87.
Swart, Gerrit, 40.
Swartwout, Roeloff, 40, 104.
Swartwout, Thomas, 76, 143.
Swedes settle on the Delaware, xiii.
Swedish settlement, 50.
Sweringen, Gerrit van, 46, 51, 108.
Symonzen, Aryaen, 184.
Talmadge, Thomas, 107.
Tapaan, 7, 8.
Taylor, Henry, 126.
Tayspil, Joannes, 6.
Teene, Isaac, 177.
Ten Broeck, Wessel, 72.
Ten Eyck, Coenraet, 177.
Tenths, Farmers of the, 36; referred to, 154.
Terneur, Daniel, 96, 97, 147.
Terri, Robert, 88, 155.
Teunissen, Cornelis, 40.
Teunissen, Gysbert, 81, 82, 145. (See *Bogaert*.)
Teunissen, Jacob, 39, 182.
Teunissen, Jan, 42.
Teunizen, Joost, 176.

Thomassen, Jelmer, 16, 23.
Throg's Neck, xiii.
Tienhoven, Adriaen van, 24, 28, 31.
Tienhoven, Cornelis van, 18, 19, 20, 24, 25, 27, 38, 115, 136, 137, 138, 150, 151, 152, 153, 154, 155, 174.
Tilje, Jan, 81.
Tilton, John, 85, 105.
Timmerman, Paulus, 2, 3, 4.
Tinnecum, 50, 102.
Tobacco inspectors, 115.
Toe, Samuel, 87.
Tomassen, Jan, 68, 69. (See *Van Dyck*.)
Tomazen, Teunis, 179.
Tonneman, Peter, 20, 21, 41, 42, 154, 155, 162.
Toorn, William, 88.
Topping Thomas, 90.
Torkillus, Reorus, 121.
Town clerks, 103.
Town crier, 112.
Town treasurers, 109.
Townsend, John, 88, 93.
Townsend, Roger, 166.
Tounsen, Thomas, 95, 168.
Truy, Philip de, 109.
Tulp, Nicholas, 6.
Turnkey, 112.
Twelve men, the, 52.
Tysen, Claes, 178, 181.
Underhill, John xiv, xvi, 15, 44, 54, 88, 160.
Underhill, Petronella, 38.
Upland, 47.
Vaile, Thomas, 98.
Valckenier, Gillis, 6.
Valentine, Richard, 110.
Van Aecken, Jan Kostersen, 71.
Van Bael, Jan Hendricks, 71.
Van Baerle, David, 1, 2, 3, 4, 5.
Van Beeck, Isaac, 1, 2, 3,
Van Brugge, Carel, 26, 27, 28, 33, 48, 106, 154, 155, 164, 174.
Van Brugge, Jan Gillisen, 174.
Van Brugh, Johannes, 60, 61, 62, 63, 67, 163, 165, 166, 167.
Van Brugh, Johannes Pietersen, 62, 63, 136, 175. (See *Verbrugge*.)
Van Brunt, Rutger Joosten, 80.

INDEX. 197

Van Cleef, Jan, 148.
Vander Beeck, Paulus, 33, 36, 117, 125, 143, 176.
Van den Bergh, Peter Jansen, 126.
Vander Capelle, Hendrick, 8, 17.
Vander Donck, Adriaen, xiv xv, xvi, 8, 16, 39, 56, 122, 136. 150.
Vandergrist, Jacob L., 116, 180.
Vandergrist, Johannes L., 116.
Vandergrist, Paulus Leenderts, 16, 17, 23, 57, 59, 60, 61, 66, 115, 141, 142, 143, 144, 150, 151, 152, 161, 162.
Vander Linde, Peter, 116, 125, 130.
Vander Sluys, Andries, 132.
Vander Spiegel, Lourens, 64.
Vander Veen, Peter Cornelissen, 65, 156, 175.
Vander Veen, Walewyn, 123.
Vander Vin, Hendrick Jansen, 62, 103.
Vander Walle, Hendrick, 29.
Van de Water, Jacobus, 26, 165, 168, 169.
Van Dyck, Cornelis, 71.
Van Dyck, Gregorius, 46.
Van Dyck, Hendrick, 13, 16, 17, 18, 38, 174.
Van Dyck, Jan Tomassen, 80, 81.
Van Elst. (See *Gaicheus*.)
Van Gheel, Maximilian, 60, 151.
Van Ham, Jan Jansen, 178.
Van Hoorn, Jan Cornelissen, 178. (See *Cornelissen*.)
Van Loon, Nicholas, 6.
Van Nes, Abraham, 108, 123.
Van Nes, Peter Petersen, 144.
Van Rensselaer, Jeremias, 136, 147.
Van Renselaer, Kiliaen, 7.
Van Schaaick, Goosen Gerritsen, 69. (See *Gerritsen*.)
Van Twiller, Wouter, 9.
Van Vleeck, Tielman, 46, 100, 123.
Van Vorst, Cornelis, 49.
Van Vorst, Joris, 183.
Varlet, Abram, 29, 164,
Varlet, Nicholas, 32, 35, 138.
Varrevanger, Jacob Hendricks, 124, 125, 128, 180.
Vedder, Herman, 71.
Vendue masters. 114.
Verbeeck, Jan, 67, 68, 69, 70, 71, 147.
Verbraack, C. J., 108.

Verbrugge, Johannes Pietersen, 66. (See *Van Brugh*.)
Verdon, Thomas, 75.
Verdonck, Thomas, 146.
Verhulst, William, 9.
Verleth, Nicolaes, 162, 182.
Verplanck, Abram, 181.
Verplanck, Gelyn, 64, 165, 168.
Verstius, William, 130.
Verveelen, Johannes, 97, 99, 107, 147.
Veryn, Jan Jansen, 166.
Videt, Jean, 176.
Vincent, Adrian, 177.
Vinge, Jan, 61, 62, 63, 174.
Virginia, xix, 35, 138.
Volck, Israel Bensen, 111.
Volckerzen, Hendrick, 183.
Voocht, Gillis de, 134.
Voorhees, Coert Stevensen van, 147, 149.
Vos, Balthazar, 80.
Vos, Hans, 39.
Vos, Nicolas, 164.
Vosch, Balthazar, 146.
Vreucht, Peter, 125.
Vries, Reynier Gerritsen, 183.
Waalboght, xiii.
Waldron, Resolved, 39, 41, 42, 97, 111, 134, 138, 180.
Walingen, Jacob, 53.
Walker, Zachariah, 120.
Wallingh, Jacob, 182.
Walraven, Thomas, 135.
Wampum, xiii.
Wantenaar, Albert Cornelissen, 73, 74, 75, 145, 147, 154.
Ward, John, 101.
Wardill, Eleakin, 101.
Washburn, William, 91, 143.
Waters, Edward, 98.
Webber, Wolfert, 97.
Weigh house, 33, 34, 35, 36.
Weights and measures, .nspectors of, 116.
Welius, Everardus, 119.
Wendel, Evert, 67, 70.
Werckhoven, Cornelis van, 8, 18, 19, 141, 142.
Wessels, David, 126.
Wessels, Harman, 126.
Wessels, Mettie, 182.

198 INDEX.

Wessels, Warnaer, 32, 33, 34, 35, 36, 116, 175.
Westchester, xiii, xv, xvii, xviii., xix, 41, 97, 107, 121, 154, 166.
Westerhout, Adriaen Jansen van, 135.
Westerhout, Jan Jansen, 135.
Wharton, William, 37.
Wheeler, Thomas, 41, 97.
Whitehead, Daniel, 91.
Whiteman, Joseph, 95.
Whiteman, Nathan, 99.
Whiting, Mr., 139.
Whorekill, 47, 51, 102, 156.
Wickendam, William, 120.
Wil, Lourens Cornelisen, 175.
Wilburch, Hilletje, 128.
Wildie, Richard, 90.
Wilkins, William, 82, 83, 84, 143.
Willemsen, Aert, 183.
Willemsen, Hendrick, 113, 116, 135, 177.
Willemsen, Jan, 52, 99.
Willemsen, Reynier, 113.
Willemsen, William, 77.

Willemstadt, xx, 71, 123, 167. (See *Fort Orange*.)
Willett, Thomas, 151, 152, 155, 159.
Wilmerdonx, Abr., 2, 3, 4, 5.
Wiltbanck, Harmanus, 102.
Wiltwyck, xix, 71, 147.
Windmill, Comptroller of the, 25.
Wisselpenningh, Rynier, 181.
Wissinck, Jacob Elbertsen, 11, 12.
Witsen, C., 3, 4.
Wolsey, George, 113.
Wood, Jonas, 95.
Wood, William, 105.
Woodbridge, 45, 169.
Woodhil, Richard, 95, 148.
Wouterzen, Aryaen, 178.
Wouterzen, Egbert, 181.
Wright, Nicolas, 95.
Wyncoop, Cornelis, 72.
Yonkers, xiv.
York, duke of, xx.
Zeeuw, Jan Cornelissen de. 81, 82.
Zetskoorn, Abelius, 121.
Zyll, Abraham van, 23.
Zyperus, Machiel, 118.

www.ingramcontent.com/pod-product-compliance
Lightning Source LLC
Chambersburg PA
CBHW050145170426
43197CB00011B/1969